RECOL[...]

Jersey Prison Ship

BY ALBERT GREENE
(From the Manuscript of Capt. Thomas Dring, Prisoner)

APPLEWOOD BOOKS
Distributed by The Globe Pequot Press

Recollections of the Jersey Prison Ship was first published in 1829.

ISBN 0-918222-92-3

Thank you for purchasing an Applewood Book.
Applewood reprints from America's lively classics—
books from the past which are still of interest to
modern readers—subjects such as cooking,
gardening, money, travel, nature, sports, and
history. Applewood Books are distributed by
The Globe Pequot Press of Chester, CT. For a
free copy of our current catalog, please write to
Applewood Books, c/o The Globe Pequot Press,
P.O. Box Q, Chester, CT 06412.

10 9 8 7 6 5 4 3 2 1

Library of Congress Cataloging-in-Publication Data
Dring, Thomas, 1758-1825.
    Recollections of the Jersey prison ship: from the manuscript of
Capt. Thomas Dring prisoner / by Albert Greene.
            p.   cm.
    Originally published: H.H. Brown, 1829.
    ISBN 0-918222-92-3 : $8.95
    1. Dring, Thomas, 1758-1825. 2. United States—History—
Revolution, 1775-1783—Prisoners and prisons. 3. United
States—History—Revolution, 1775-1783—Personal narratives.
4. Jersey (Prison-ship) 5. Prisoners of war—United States—
Biography.   6. Prisoners of war—Great Britain—Biogra-
phy.   I. Greene, Albert G. (Albert Gorton), 1802-1868.   II.
Title.
 E281.D79   1992   92-6512
 973.3'71—dc20   CIP

RECOLLECTIONS

OF THE

JERSEY PRISON-SHIP;

Taken and prepared for publication from the original manuscript of the late

CAPTAIN THOMAS DRING,

OF PROVIDENCE, R. I.

ONE OF THE PRISONERS.

BY ALBERT G. GREENE.

" It was there, that hunger and thirst and disease, and all the contumely which cold-hearted cruelty could bestow, sharpened every pang of death. Misery there wrung every fibre that could feel, before she gave the blow of grace, which sent the sufferer to eternity." — *Russell's Oration.*

Providence:

PUBLISHED BY H. H. BROWN.

1829.

PREFACE.

In presenting the following narrative to the public, it is deemed proper that it should be accompanied with a brief notice of the individual from whose memory these Recollections were drawn; and with some account of the materials left by him, from which this work has been compiled.

Excepting the events described in this volume, his biography would afford but few incidents of sufficient importance to excite public attention. The prime of his life was spent in active employment upon the ocean, and his remaining years were passed in the avocations of the quiet and industrious citizen. The events of the latter yield no themes for comment; and the former, although not without its scenes of peril and adventure, affords nothing which here requires to be recorded.

Capt. Thomas Dring was born in the town of Newport (R. I.), on the third day of August, 1758.

He was therefore in his twenty-fifth year when the events occurred which form the subject of the present volume.   After the termination of his confinement on board the *Jersey*, he entered the merchant service, and soon attained the command of a ship.   He sailed from the port of Providence for many years, and was well known as an able and experienced officer.   In the year 1803 he retired from his nautical profession and soon after established himself in business in Providence, where he resided during the remainder of his life.   He died on the eighth day of August, 1825, aged 67 years; leaving many by whom his memory will long be preserved, as a kind relative, an intelligent and industrious citizen, a worthy and an honest man.

The original manuscript from which the facts contained in the following pages have been taken, was written in the year 1824.   Although it was finished but a few months previous to his decease, his faculties were then perfect and unimpaired, and his memory remained clear and unclouded, even in regard to the most minute facts.   To those who were personally acquainted with Capt. Dring, his character affords sufficient assurance of the correctness of his narrative.

His manuscript is a closely written folio of about sixty pages, containing a great number of interesting

facts, thrown together, without m uch regard to style
or to chronological order.   Not being intended for
publication, at least in the form in which he left it, he
appears to have bestowed but little regard on the language in which his facts were described, or on the
arrangement or connexion in which they were placed.
His only aim, indeed, appears to have been, to com-
mit faithfully to paper his recollections of all the
principal events which transpired during his own confinement, and the material circumstances in relation to
the general treatment of the prisoners.   His writing
accordingly abounds with repetitions of not only the
most important, but even of the most minute occurrences.   These, although they add value to a manuscript like his, proving the strength and accuracy of
his memory, by the perfect accordance of his descriptions of the same facts, made at different times; still
in a published book they could be viewed but as useless redundancies, at least.

The manuscript has been sought for and eagerly
perused by several gentlemen of high respectability,
who were either prisoners on board the *Jersey*, or
placed in situations where they had ample opportuni-
ties of being acquainted with the facts.   They have
uniformly borne testimony to the correctness of its
details ; but have been, at the same time, unanimous

in the opinion that a perfect and complete revision of
its style and arrangement was absolutely required.

It was, in fact, necessary that the work should not
merely be revised, but rewritten, before its publication.   To do this in a proper manner was no easy
task.   It was necessary to divide the narrative into
distinct and separate chapters ; and consequently, to
transpose and connect detached facts under their
proper heads, in order to produce a degree of uniform-
ity in the whole.   But while the circumstances not
only allowed, but required, full liberty to be taken
with the language and arrangement of the narrative,
still nothing has been added, and no fact or occurrence
of the least importance has been omitted.   Throughout the whole work, the most scrupulous care has
been taken that the incidents as here pourtrayed,
should exactly agree with the descriptions of Capt.
Dring; and also, that they should be so set forth as
to appear neither of more nor less importance than
he appears to have attached to them, while writing
his manuscript.

CONTENTS.

NOTE.

I⊤ may be proper to mention, that the Engraving which accompanies this volume is copied from an original sketch made by Capt. DRING, and attached to his Manuscript. The References are given almost in his own words.

Fig. 1.

THE JERSEY PRISON SHIP,

AS MOORED AT THE WALLABOUT NEAR LONG ISLAND, IN THE YEAR 1782.

THE

JERSEY PRISON-SHIP.

GENERAL DESCRIPTION

OF THE

JERSEY PRISON-SHIP,

WITH REFERENCES TO THE PLATES.

THE *Jersey* was originally a British ship of the line. She was rated and registered as a sixty-four gun ship, but had usually mounted seventy-four guns. At the commencement of the American Revolution, being an old vessel, and proving to be much decayed, she was entirely dismantled, and soon after was moored in the East River at New-York, and converted into a store-ship. In the year 1780, she was fitted as a prison-ship, and was used for that purpose during the remainder of the war. Fears having been very naturally felt that the destructive contagion by which so many of her unfortunate inmates had been swept away might spread to the shore, she was, in consequence. removed, and moored, with chain cables, at the Wallabout, a solitary and unfrequented place on the shore of Long-Island. She had been dismantled, and her rudder unhung. Her only spars were the bowsprit, a derrick for taking in supplies of water, &c., and a flag-staff at the stern. Her port-holes had all been closed and strongly fastened, and two tiers of small holes cut through her sides. These holes were about ten feet apart, each being about twenty inches square, and guarded by two strong bars of iron, crossing it at right angles; thus leaving four contracted spaces, which admitted light by day, and served as breathing holes at night. The interior construction and arrangement of the ship, will be clearly understood by an examination of the Engraving, illustrated by the following references.

REFERENCES TO THE PLATE.

FIGURE 1.—*Exterior View of the Ship.*

1. The Flag Staff, which was seldom used, and only for signals.
2. A Canvass Awning or Tent, used by the guards in warm weather.
3. The Quarter Deck, with its barricado about ten feet high, with a door and loop holes on each side.
4. The Ship's Officers' Cabin, under the quarter deck.
5. Accommodation Ladder, on the starboard side, for the use of the Ship's officers.
6. The Steerage, occupied by the sailors belonging to the Ship.

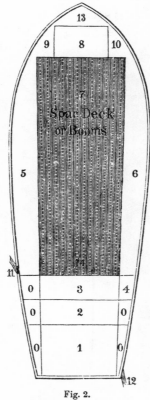

Fig. 2.

THE GUN DECK,

WITH ITS APARTMENTS.

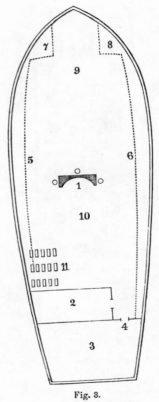

Fig. 3.

THE MIDDLE DECK.

*The arrangement of the Lower Deck
(was similar, but without Bunks.)*

7. The Cook Room for the Ship's crew and guards.
8. The Suttler's Room, where articles were sold to the prisoners, and delivered to them through an opening in the bulk head.
9. The Upper Deck and Spar Deck, where the prisoners were occasionally allowed to walk.
10. The Gangway Ladder, on the larboard side, for the prisoners.
11. The Derrick, on the starboard side, for taking in water, &c., &c.
12. The Galley, or Great Copper, under the forecastle, where the provisions were cooked for the prisoners.
13. The Gun Room, occupied by those prisoners who were officers.
14, 15. Hatchways leading below, where the prisoners were confined.
17, 18. Between decks, where the prisoners were confined by night.
19. The Bowsprit.
20. Chain Cables, by which the Ship was moored.

FIGURE 2.—*The Gun Deck, with its Apartments.*

1. Cabin.	9, 10. The Cook's quarters.
2. Steerage.	11. The Gangway Ladder.
3. Cook Room.	12. The Officers' Ladder.
4. Suttler's Room.	13. Working Party.
5, 6. Gangways.	14. The Barricado.
7. The Booms.	o o o Store Rooms.
8. The Galley.	

FIGURE 3.—*The Upper Deck, between Decks.*

1. The Hatchway Ladder, leading to the lower deck, railed round on three sides.
2. The Steward's Room, from which the prisoners received their daily allowance, through an opening in the partition.
3. The Gun Room, occupied by those prisoners who were officers.
4 Door of the Gun Room.

5, 6, 7, 8. The arrangement of the prisoners' chests and boxes, which were ranged along, about ten feet from the sides of the Ship, leaving a vacant space, where the messes assembled.

9, 10. The middle of the deck, where many of the prisoners' hammocks were hung at night, but always taken down in the morning, to afford room for walking.

11. Bunks, on the larboard side of the deck, for the reception of the sick.

RECOLLECTIONS, &c.

———◆———

CHAPTER I.

OUR CAPTURE.

" 'The various horrors of these hulks to tell,
" Where want and woe, where pain and penance dwell ;
" Where Death in ten-fold vengeance holds his reign,
" And injured ghosts, yet unavenged, complain,
" This be my task."———

FRENEAU.

AMONG the varied events of the war of the American Revolution, there are few circumstances which have left a deeper impression on the public mind, than those connected with the cruel and vindictive treatment which was experienced by those of our unfortunate countrymen whom the fortune of war had placed on board the Prison-Ships of the enemy. Still, among the vague and indistinct narrations which have been made, (although in almost every instance falling short of the dreadful reality,) but few statements have been given to the world in an authentic form; and these have been for the most part relations of detached facts and circumstances, rather than such distinct and connected accounts as might afford the reader a correct view of all the important facts in relation to the subject.

Indeed, most of those who have spoken and who could have written of these facts with the fidelity of eye witnesses, have already passed beyond the scenes of earth; and while living, had but slight inducements to devote the necessary time and labour to record the history of their former sufferings.

Hence, so little that is authentic, has ever been published upon the subject, and so scanty are the materials for information respecting it, which have as yet been given to the rising generations of our country, that it has already become a matter of doubt, even among many of the intelligent and well-informed of our young citizens, whether the tales of the Prison-Ships, such as they have been told, have not been exaggerated beyond the reality. They have not been exaggerated. Much of the truth has, indeed, been told; but not one half the detail of its horrors has ever been pourtrayed.

But the period has now arrived, which requires that some authentic record should be made, in order that the truth of these events shall not remain a subject of doubt and uncertainty. And so few of those who suffered in these terrific abodes remain alive, that as a matter of precaution, it seems to be required that some one possessing actual knowledge of the facts, should embody them in a form more permanent than the tales of tradition, and more detailed than can appear on the page of the general historian.

All the important occurrences of that eventful period, all which conspired to give its peculiar character to the lengthened contest, or which had an effect in advancing or retarding its issue, every thing which tends to shew the spirit with which it was conducted on either side, is certainly worthy of record and of remembrance. In this light, I view the facts in relation to the treatment of the American seamen on board the British Prison-Ships.   These facts are a portion of our country's history ; and that history would not be complete, one of its deepest lessons would be lost, were the page which bears the record of these facts, to be obliterated.

The principal motive of the writer of the following pages, in recording the facts which they contain, was originally to strengthen his recollection of the particulars relative to the events which he has described.   Although nearly half a century has elapsed, since these events occurred, yet so indelible was the impression which they left on his mind, that they seem in all their details, but as the things of yesterday ; and if memory remains to him, they will go with him, in all their freshness, to the grave.

In a very short time, there will be not one being on the face of the earth, who can, from his own knowledge, relate this tale ; though many still live, who although not among the sufferers, yet well know the truth of the circumstances which I have written.

The number of those who perished on board the prison and hospital ships at the Wallabout,

has never been, and never can be known. It has
been ascertained, however, with as much pre-
cision as the nature of the case will admit, that
more than TEN THOUSAND died on board the
Jersey, and the hospital ships *Scorpion*, *Strombolo*, and *Hunter*. Thousands there suffered,
and pined and died, whose names have never
been known by their countrymen. They died
where no eye could admire their fortitude, no
tongue could praise their devotion to their country's cause.

For years, the very name of "the old *Jersey*,"
seemed to strike a terror to the hearts of those
whose necessities required them to venture upon
the ocean; the mortality which prevailed on
board her was well known throughout the country; and to be confined within her dungeons,
was considered equal to a sentence of death,
from which but little hope of escape remained.

It was my hard fortune, in the course of the
war, to be twice confined on board the prison-
ships of the enemy. I was first immured in the
year 1779, on board the *Good Hope*, then lying
in the North River, opposite the city of New-

2

York ; but after a confinement of more than four months, I succeeded in making my escape to the Jersey shore.   Afterwards, in the year 1782, I was again captured and conveyed on board the *Jersey*, where for nearly five months, I was a witness and a partaker of the unspeakable sufferings of that wretched class of American prisoners, who were there taught the utmost extent of human misery.

I am now far advanced in years, and am the only survivor (with the exception of two) of a crew of sixty-five men.   I often pass some descendant of one of my old companions in captivity ; and the recollection comes fresh to my mind, that his father was my comrade and fellow-sufferer in prison ; that I saw him breathe his last upon the deck of the *Jersey*, and assisted at his interment at the Wallabout ; circumstances probably wholly unknown to the person, the sight of whom had excited the recollection.

In the month of May, 1782, I sailed from Providence (Rhode-Island), as Master's Mate, on board a privateer called the *Chance*.   This was a new vessel, on her first cruise. She was owned in Providence, by Messrs. Clarke & Nightingale, and manned chiefly from that place and vicinity. She was commanded by Capt. Daniel Aborn, mounted twelve six pound cannon; and sailed with a complement of about sixty-five men. She was officered as follows, viz:

Daniel Aborn, of Pawtuxet, R. I.	Commander.
John Tillinghast, Providence,	First Lieut.
James Hawkins, Pawtuxet,	Second do.
Sylvester Rhodes, do.	Sailing-master.
Thomas Dring, Providence,	Master's Mate.
Joseph Bowen, do.	Surgeon.
Robert Carver, do.	Gunner.
Joseph Arnold, do.	Carpenter.
John W. Gladding, do.	Prize Master.

The names of several other officers, in inferior stations, I do not recollect at this distant period of time.

Our cruise was but a short one: for in a few days after sailing, we were captured by the British ship of war *Belisarius*, Capt. Graves, of twenty-six guns. We were captured in the night, and our crew having been conveyed on board the enemy's ship, were put in irons the next morning. During the next day, the *Belisarius* made two other prizes, a privateer brig from New-London or Stonington (Conn.), called the *Samson*, of twelve guns, commanded by Capt. Brooks, and a merchant schooner from Warren (R. I.), commanded by Capt. Charles Collins. The crews of these two vessels, except the principal officers, were also put in irons. These captures were all made on soundings, south of Long-Island. The putting their prisoners in irons was a necessary precaution on the part of the captors. We were kept confined in the cable-tier of the ship, but were occasionally permitted to go on deck during the day in small parties. The *Belisarius*, then having on board upwards of one hundred and thirty prisoners, soon made her way for New-York, in company with her prizes.

Our situation on board this ship was not, indeed, a very enviable one; but uncomfortable as it was, it was far preferable to that in which we soon expected to be placed, and which we soon found it was our doom to experience. The ship dropped her anchor, abreast of the city, and signals were immediately made that she had prisoners on board. Soon after, two large gondolas or boats came alongside, in one of which was seated the notorious David Sproat, the Commissary of Prisoners. This man was an American Refugee, universally detested for the cruelty of his conduct and the insolence of his manners.

We were then called on deck, and having been released from our irons, were ordered into the boats. This being accomplished, we put off from the ship, under a guard of marines, and proceeded towards our much dreaded place of confinement, which was not then in sight. As we passed along the Long-Island shore, against the tide, our progress was very slow. The prisoners were ordered, by Sproat, to apply themselves to the oars; but not feeling any particular anxiety to expedite our progress, we declined obeying the command. His only reply was, " I'll soon fix you, my lads."

We at length doubled a point, and came in view of the Wallabout, where lay before us the black hulk of the old *Jersey*, with her satellites, the three Hospital Ships; to which Sproat pointed in an exulting manner, and said, " There, Rebels,

3

there is the *cage* for you." Oh! how I wished to be standing alone with that inhuman wretch upon the green turf, at that moment!

As he spoke, my eye was instantly turned from the dreaded hulk: but a single glance had shown us a multitude of human beings moving upon her upper deck. Many were on her bow-sprit, for the purpose, as I afterwards learned, of getting without the limits.

It was then nearly sunset: and before we were alongside, every man, except the sentinels on the gangway, had disappeared. Previous to their being sent below, some of the prisoners, seeing us approaching, waved their hats, as if they would say, Approach us not: and we soon found fearful reason for the warning.

CHAPTER II.

THE FIRST NIGHT ON BOARD.

" Hail, dark abode ! what can with thee compare —
" Heat, sickness, famine, death, and stagnant air.
" Pandora's box, from whence all mischiefs flow,
" Here *real* found, torments mankind anew.
" Swift, from the guarded decks, we rushed along,
" And vainly sought repose, so vast our throng.
" Three hundred wretches here, denied all light,
" In crowded mansions, pass th' infernal night.
" Some, for a bed their tatter'd vestments join;
" And some on chests, and some on floors, recline.
" Shut from the blessings of the evening air,
" Pensive we lay, with mingled corpses there.
" Meagre and wan, and scorched with heat below,
" We *looked* like ghosts, ere death had *made* us so."

FRENEAU.

WE had now reached the accommodation ladder, which led to the gangway on the larboard
side of the *Jersey ;* and my station in the boat,
as she hauled alongside, was exactly opposite to
one of the air-ports in the side of the ship.

From this aperture proceeded a strong current of foul vapor, of a kind to which I had been before accustomed, while confined on board the *Good Hope;* the peculiarly disgusting smell of which I then recollected, after a lapse of three years. This was, however, far more foul and loathsome than any thing which I had ever met with on board that ship, and produced a sensation of nausea far beyond my powers of description.

Here, while waiting for orders to ascend on board, we were addressed by some of the prisoners, from the air-ports. We could not, however, discern their features, as it had now become so dark that we could not distinctly see any object in the interior of the ship. After some questions, whence we came, and respecting the manner of our capture, one of the prisoners said to me, that it was " a lamentable thing to see so many young men in full strength, with the flush of health upon their countenances, about to enter that infernal place of abode." He then added, in a tone and manner but little fitted to afford us much consolation, — " Death has no relish for such skeleton carcasses as we are, but he will now have a feast upon you fresh comers."

After lanterns had been lighted on board, for our examination, we ascended the accommodation ladder, to the upper deck, and passed through the barricado door ; where we were examined, and our bags of clothes inspected. These we were permitted to retain, provided they contained no money or weapons of any kind.

After each man had given his name and the capacity in which he had served on board the vessel in which he was captured, and the same had been duly registered, we were directed to pass through the other barricado door, on the starboard side, down the ladder leading to the main hatchway. I was detained but a short time with the examination, and was permitted to take my bag of clothes with me below ; and passing down the hatchway, which was still open, through a guard of soldiers, I found myself among the wretched and disgusting multitude, a prisoner on board the *Jersey*.

The gratings were soon after placed over the hatchways, and fastened down for the night ; and

4

I seated myself on the deck, holding my bag
with a firm grasp, fearful of losing it among the
crowd.   I had now ample time to reflect on the
horrors of the scene, and to consider the prospect before me.   It was impossible to find one
of my former shipmates in the darkness; and I
had, of course, no one with whom to speak
during the long hours of that dreadful night.
Surrounded by I knew not whom, except that
they were beings as wretched as myself; with
dismal sounds meeting my ears from every
direction; a nauseous and putrid atmosphere
filling my lungs at every breath; and a stifled
and suffocating heat, which almost deprived me
of sense, and even of life.

Previous to leaving the boat, I had put on several additional articles of apparel for the purpose
of security; but I was soon compelled to dis-
encumber myself of these; and was willing to
hazard their loss, for a relief from the intolerable
heat.

The thought of sleep did not enter my mind:
and at length, discovering a glimmering of light
through the iron gratings of one of the air-ports,

I felt that it would be indeed a luxury, if I could but obtain a situation near that place, in order to gain one breath of the exterior air. Clenching my hand firmly around my bag, which I dared not leave, I began to advance towards the side of the ship; but was soon greeted with the curses and imprecations of those who were lying on the deck, and whom I had disturbed in attempting to pass over them. I however persevered, and at length arrived near the desired spot; but found it already occupied, and no persuasion could induce a single individual to relinquish his place for a moment.

Thus I passed the first dreadful night, waiting with sorrowful forebodings for the coming day. The dawn at length appeared, but came only to present new scenes of wretchedness, disease, and woe. I found myself surrounded by a crowd of strange and unknown forms, with the lines of death and famine upon their faces. My former shipmates were all lost and mingled among the multitude, and it was not until we were permitted to ascend the deck, at eight o'clock, that I could discern a single individual whom I had ever seen before. Pale and meagre, the throng came upon deck ; to view, for a few moments, the morning sun, and then, to descend again, to pass another day of misery and wretchedness.

CHAPTER III.

THE FIRST DAY.

" Dull flew the hours, 'till from the East displayed,
" Sweet morn dispelled the horrors of the shade.
" On every side, dire objects met the sight,
" And pallid forms, and murders of the night.
" The dead were past their pain ; the living groan,
" Nor dare to hope another morn their own.
" But, what to them is morn's delightful ray ?
" Sad and distressful as the close of day.
" O'er distant streams, appears the dewy green,
" And leafy trees on mountain tops, are seen.
" But they no groves nor grassy mountains tread,
" Marked for a longer journey to the dead."

FRENEAU.

AFTER passing the weary and tedious night, to whose accumulated horrors I have but slightly alluded, I was permitted to ascend to the upper deck, where other objects, even more disgusting and loathsome, met my view. I found myself surrounded by a motley crew of wretches with

fresh air.   Among them, I saw one ruddy and
healthful countenance, and recognized the features of one of my late fellow prisoners on board
the *Belisarius*.   But how different did he appear
from the group around him, who had here been
doomed to combat with disease and death.   Men,
who, shrunken and decayed as they stood around
him, had been, but a short time before, as strong,
as healthful and as vigorous as himself.   Men,
who had breathed the pure breezes of the ocean,
or danced lightly in the flower-scented air of the
meadow and the hill ; and had from thence been
hurried into the pent-up air of a crowded prison-
ship, pregnant with putrid fever, foul with deadly
contagion ; here to linger out the tedious and
weary day, the disturbed and anxious night ; to
count over the days and weeks and months of
a wearying and degrading captivity, unvaried but
by new scenes of painful suffering, and new inflictions of remorseless cruelty : their brightest
hope and their daily prayer, that death would not
long delay to release them from their torments.

In the wretched groups around me, I saw but
too faithful a picture of our own almost certain

fate; and found that all which we had been taught to fear of this terrible place of abode, was more than realized.

During the night, in addition to my other sufferings, I had been tormented with what I supposed to be vermin; and on coming upon deck, I found that a black silk handkerchief, which I wore around my neck, was completely spotted with them. Although this had often been mentioned as one of the miseries of the place, yet as I had never before been in a situation to witness any thing of the kind, the sight made me shudder; as I knew, at once, that so long as I should remain on board, these loathsome creatures would be my constant companions and unceasing tormentors.

The next disgusting object which met my sight was a man suffering with the small pox; and in a few minutes, I found myself surrounded by many others, labouring under the same disease, in every stage of its progress.

As I had never had the small pox, it became necessary that I should be inoculated; and there being no proper person on board to perform the operation, I concluded to act as my own physician. On looking about me, I soon found a man in the proper stage of the disease, and desired him to favor me with some of the matter for the purpose. He readily complied; observing that it was a necessary precaution on my part, and that my situation was an excellent one in regard to *diet*, as I might depend upon finding that *extremely moderate*.

The only instrument which I could procure for the purpose of inoculation, was a common pin. With this, having scarified the skin of my hand, between the thumb and fore-finger, I applied the matter and bound up my hand. The next morning, I found that the wound had begun to fester; a sure symptom that the application had taken effect.

Many of my former shipmates took the same precaution, and were inoculated during the day. In my case, the disorder came on but lightly, and its progress was favourable; and without the least medical advice or attention, by the blessing of Divine Providence, I soon recovered.

Since that time, more than forty years have

passed away; but the scar on my hand is still
plainly to be seen.   I often look upon it, when
alone, and it brings fresh to my recollection, the
fearful scene in which I was then placed, the
circumstances by which it was attended, and the
feelings which I then experienced.

As the prisoners sent from the *Belisarius* had
not been formed into regular messes, and numbered according to the regulations of the ship,
they were unable to draw their share of provisions for the day, in time for cooking.   They had
now all fasted for nearly twenty-four hours; and
knew not in what manner to obtain a morsel of
food.   For my own part, it fortunately happened,
that at the time of our capture, I had taken the
precaution to put a few biscuit into my bag; and
not having had occasion to use them while on
board the *Belisarius*, I was now furnished with
the means of satisfying, in some degree, the
cravings of my own hunger; and was also enabled to distribute a portion of bread among some
of my comrades.

In the course of the day, after the regulations
of the ship had been made known to us, we

6

divided ourselves into messes of six men each;
and on the next morning, we drew our scanty
pittance of food with the rest of our companions.

CHAPTER IV.

THE GUN ROOM AND MESSES.

" But, such a train of endless woes abound,
" So many mischiefs in these hulks are found,
" That, of them all, the memory to prolong,
" Would swell too high the horrors of our song.
" Hunger and thirst, to work our woe, combine,
" And mouldy bread, and flesh of rotten swine;
" The mangled carcass, and the battered brain,
" The doctor's poison, and the captain's cane,
" The soldier's musket, and the steward's debt,
" The evening shackle, and the noon-day threat."

FRENEAU.

ON the arrival of prisoners on board the *Jersey*, the first thing necessary to be done was, as soon as possible, to form, or be admitted into, some regular *mess*. On the day of a prisoner's arrival, it was impossible for him to procure any food; and even on the second day, he could not procure any, in time to have it cooked. No matter how long he had fasted, nor how acute might be his sufferings from hunger and privation; his

petty tyrants would on no occasion deviate from
their rule of delivering the prisoner's morsel at
a particular hour, and at no other. And the poor,
half famished wretch must absolutely wait until
the coming day, before his pittance of food could
be boiled with that of his fellow captives. It
was therefore most prudent for a newly arrived
prisoner, to gain admittance into some old established mess, (which was not attended with much
difficulty, as death was daily providing vacan-
cies;) for he would thereby be associated with
those who were acquainted with the mode of
procuring their allowance in time; and be also
protected from many impositions, to which as a
stranger he otherwise would be liable during the
first days of his confinement.

The cruel tyrants, to whose petty sway we
were subjected on board this hulk, knew no distinction among their prisoners. Whether taken
on the land or on the ocean, in arms, or from
our own firesides, it was the same to them. No
matter in what rank or capacity a prisoner might
have been known before his capture, no distinction was here made; we were " all *Rebels.*"

Our treatment, our fare, its allowance and its quality were the same. They did not, of course, interfere in our private arrangements; but left us to manage our affairs in our own way.

The extreme after part of the ship, between decks, was called the *Gun Room*. (See the Plate, Figure 3.) Although no distinction was made by our masters, yet those among the prisoners who had been officers previous to their capture, had taken possession of this room as their own place of abode; and from custom, it was considered as belonging exclusively to them. As an officer, I found my way into this apartment; and with such of my late companions as had been officers, was received with civility by those who were already in possession of it; who humanely tendered us such little services as were in their power to offer. We soon became incorporated with them; and having formed ourselves into messes, as nearly as possible according to our grades, we were considered as a part of this family of sufferers.

The different messes of the prisoners were all numbered; and every morning, at nine o'clock,

the Steward and his assistants having taken their
station at the window in the bulk head of the
Steward's room, (See the Plate, Figure 3,) the
bell was rung, and the messes called in rotation.

An individual belonging to each mess stood
ready in order to be in time to answer when its
number was called.   As the number of each
mess was spoken, its allowance was handed from
the window, to the person waiting to receive it;
the rations being all prepared previous to the
hour of delivery.   The prisoner must receive
for his mess, whatever was offered; and be its
quantity or quality what it might, no alteration
or change was ever allowed.   We as prisoners,
were allowed each day for *six* men, what was
equal in quantity to the rations of *four* men at
full allowance.   That is, each prisoner was furnished in quantity with two thirds of the allowance of a seaman in the British Navy; which was
as follows:

On Sunday,	1 lb. of biscuit, 1 lb. of pork, and half a pint of peas.
" *Monday*,	1 lb. of biscuit, 1 pint of oat meal, 2 ounces of butter.
" *Tuesday*,	1 lb. of biscuit and two lbs. of beef.
" *Wednesday*,	1 1-2 lbs of flour, and two ounces of suet.
" *Thursday*,	The same as Sunday.
" *Friday*,	The same as Monday.
" *Saturday*,	The same as Tuesday.

Hence, as prisoners, whenever we had our due, we received, as they said, two thirds of the ordinary allowance of their own seamen ; and even this was of a very inferior quality. We never received any butter; but in its stead, they gave us a substance which they called sweet oil. This was so rancid, and even putrid, that the smell of it, accustomed as we were to every thing foul and nauseous, was more than we could endure. We however, always received and gave it to the poor, half-starved Frenchmen who were on board ; who took it gratefully, and swallowed it with a little salt and their wormy bread. Oil of a similar quality, was given to the prisoners on board the *Good Hope*, where I was confined in 1779. There however, it was of some use to us, as we burnt it in our lamps ; being there indulged with the privilege of using lights until nine o'clock at night. But here, it was of no service ; as we were allowed on board the *Jersey*, no light or fire, on any occasion whatever.

CHAPTER V.

THE COOK'S QUARTERS.

" Why, Britain, raged thy insolence and scorn ?
" Why burst thy vengeance on the wretch forlorn ?
" The cheerless captive, to slow death consigned,
" Chilled with keen frosts, in prison glooms confined,
" Of hope bereft, by thy vile minions curst.
" With hunger famished, and consumed by thirst,
" Without one friend, — when death's last horror stung,
" Rolled the wild eye, and gnawed the anguished tongue."
HUMPHREYS.

HAVING received our daily rations, which were frequently not delivered to us in time to be boiled on the same day, we were consequently often under the necessity of fasting for the next twenty-four hours, if we had not a stock of provisions on hand; or were obliged at times to consume our food in its raw state, when the cravings of hunger could no longer be resisted.

The cooking for the great mass of the prisoners was done under the forecastle, or, as it was usually called, the Galley, in a boiler or "Great Copper," which was enclosed in brick work, about eight feet square. This copper was large enough to contain two or three hogsheads of water. It was made in a square form, and divided into two separate compartments, by a partition. In one side of the Copper, the peas and oatmeal for the prisoners were boiled, which was done in fresh water. In the other side, the meat was boiled. This side of the boiler was filled with salt water from alongside the ship; by which means, the copper became soon corroded, and consequently poisonous: the fatal consequences of which are so obvious, that I need not enlarge upon the subject.

After the daily rations had been furnished to the different messes, the portion of each mess was designated by a tally fastened to it by a string. Being thus prepared, every ear was anxiously waiting for the summons of the *Cook's bell*. As soon as this was heard to sound, the persons having charge of the different portions

of food, thronged to the Galley; and in a few
minutes after, hundreds of tallies were seen
hanging over the sides of the brick work, by
their respective strings, each eagerly watched by
someindividual of the mess, who always waited
to receive it.   The meat was suffered thus to remain in the boiler but a certain time; and when
this had elapsed, the cook's bell was again rung,
and the pittance of food must be immediately removed.   Whether sufficiently cooked, or not, it
could remain no longer.   The proportions of
peas and oat-meal belonging to each mess were
measured out from the Copper, after they were
boiled.

Among the emaciated crowd of living skele-
tons who had remained on board for any length
of time, the cook was the only person who appeared to have much flesh upon his bones.   He
perhaps contrived to obtain a greater quantity of
provisions than any of ourselves; but if they
were of the same quality with our own, it is obvious that his plumpness of appearance could not
be the result of *good living*.   He had himself
been formerly a prisoner; but seeing no pros-

pect of ever being liberated, he had entered in his present capacity; and his mates and scullions had followed his example, they having also been prisoners at first. I attributed the appearance of our Cook merely to the fact, that he was more content with his situation than any other person on board appeared to be. He indeed possessed a considerable share of good humour; and although often cursed by the prisoners (but not in his hearing) for his refusals to comply with their requests, yet considering the many applications which were made to him for favours, and the incumbrances which were around "his palace," he really displayed a degree of fortitude and forbearance far beyond what most men would have been capable of exhibiting under similar circumstances. He did, indeed, at times, when his patience was exhausted, "make the hot water fly among us;" but a reconciliation was usually effected, with but little difficulty.

In consequence of the poisonous effects produced by the use of the sea water for boiling our meat in the Great Copper, many of the different messes had obtained permission from "his

Majesty the Cook," to prepare their own rations
separate from the general mess in the great
boiler. For this purpose, a great number of
spikes and hooks had been driven into the brick
work by which the boiler was enclosed, on
which to suspend their tin kettles. As soon as
we were permitted to go on deck in the morning,
some one took the tin kettle belonging to the
mess, with as much water, and such splinters of
wood as we had been able to procure during the
previous day, and carried them to the Galley;
and there having suspended his kettle on one of
the hooks or spikes in the brick work, he stood
ready to kindle his little fire, as soon as the cook
or his mates would permit it to be done. It required but little fuel to boil our food in these
kettles; for their bottoms were made in a con-
cave form, and the fire was applied directly in
the centre. And let the remaining brands be
ever so small, they were all carefully quenched;
and having been conveyed below, were kept for
use on a future occasion. Much contention often
arose, through our endeavors to obtain places
round the brick work; but these disputes were

always promptly decided by the Cook, from whose mandate there was no appeal. No sooner had one prisoner completed the cooking for his mess, than another supplicant stood ready to take his place; and they thus continued to throng the Galley, during the whole time that the fire was allowed to remain under the Great Copper; unless it happened to be the pleasure of the Cook, to drive them away.

I have said that but little wood was requisite for our purpose; but the great difficulty was to procure a sufficient quantity of fresh water for this manner of cooking. The arrangement by which we effected this, was, by agreeing that each man in the mess should, during the day previous, procure and save as much water as possible; as no prisoner was ever allowed to take more than a pint, at one time, from the scuttle cask in which it was kept. Every individual was therefore obliged, each day, to save a little, for the common use of the mess, on the next morning. By this arrangement, the mess to which I belonged, had always a small quantity of fresh water in store; which we carefully kept, with a

9

few other necessaries, in a chest which we used in common.

During the whole period of my confinement, I never partook of any food which had been cooked in the Great Copper. It is to this fact, that I have always attributed, under Divine Providence, the degree of health which I preserved while on board. I was thereby also, at times, enabled to procure several necessary and comfortable things, such as tea, sugar, &c. so that wretchedly as I was situated, my condition was far preferable to that of most of my fellow sufferers; which has ever been with me, a theme of sincere and lasting gratitude to Heaven.

But terrible indeed was the condition of most of my fellow captives. Memory still brings before me those emaciated beings, moving from the Galley, with their wretched pittance of meat; each creeping to the spot where his mess were assembled, to divide it with a group of haggard and sickly creatures, their garments hanging in tatters around their meagre limbs, and the hue of death upon their care-worn faces. By these, it was consumed with their scanty remnants of bread, which was often mouldy and filled with worms. And even from this vile fare, they would rise up, in torments from the cravings of unsatisfied hunger and thirst.

No vegetables of any description were ever afforded us by our inhuman keepers. Good Heaven! what a luxury to us would then have been even a few potatoes; if but the very leavings of the swine of our country.

CHAPTER VI.

OUR SITUATION.

" Oh ! my heart sinks, my trembling eyes o'erflow,
" When memory paints the picture of their woe.
" Where my poor countrymen in bondage, wait
" The slow enfranchisement of lingering fate ;
" Greeting with groans the unwelcome night's return,
" While rage and shame their gloomy bosoms burn ;
" And chiding, every hour, the slow paced sun,
" Endure their woes till all his race was run.
" No eye to mark their sufferings with a tear,
" No friend to comfort, and no hope to cheer.
" And like the dull unpitied brutes, repair
" To stalls as wretched and as coarse a fare ;
" Thank Heaven, one day of misery was o'er,
" And sink to sleep, and wish to wake no more."

DAY.

BEFORE attempting a more minute account of
our manner of living on board the *Jersey*, it may
be proper to add a further description of the
ship. The Quarter Deck covered about one
fourth part of the upper deck, from the stern ;

and the forecastle extended from the stern, about one eighth part of the length of the upper deck. Sentinels were stationed on the gangways on each side of the upper deck leading from the quarter deck to the forecastle. These gangways were about five feet wide, and here the prisoners were allowed to pass and repass. The intermediate space from the bulk head of the quarter deck to the forecastle, was filled with long spars or booms, and called the Spar Deck. The temporary covering afforded by the spar deck, was of the greatest benefit to the prisoners; as it served to shield us from the rain and the scorching rays of the sun. It was here also that our moveables were placed while we were engaged in cleaning the lower decks. The spar deck was also the only place where we were allowed to walk; and was therefore continually crowded, through the day, by those of the prisoners who were upon deck. Owing to the great number of the prisoners, and the small space afforded us by the spar deck, it was our custom to walk, in platoons, each facing the same way, and turning at the same time. The derrick, for taking in wood, water, &c. stood on the starboard side of the spar deck. On the larboard side of the ship, was placed the accommodation ladder, leading from the gangway to the water. At the head of this ladder, a sentinel was also stationed.

The head of the accommodation ladder was near the door of the barricado, which extended across the front of the quarter deck, and projected a few feet beyond the sides of the ship. The barricado was about ten feet high, and was pierced with loop-holes for musketry; in order that the prisoners might be fired on from behind it, if occasion should require.

The regular crew of the ship consisted of a Captain, two Mates, a Steward, a Cook, and about twelve sailors. The crew of the ship had no communication whatever with the prisoners. No prisoner was ever permitted to pass through the barricado door, except when it was required that the messes should be examined and regulated; in which case, each man had to pass through, and go down between decks; and there remain, until the examination was completed.

None of the guard or of the ship's crew ever
came among the prisoners, while I was on board.
I never saw one of her officers or men, except
when they were passing in their boat, to or from
the stern ladder.

On the two decks below, where we were confined at night, our chests, boxes and bags were ar-
ranged in two lines along the deck, about ten feet
distant from the sides of the ship; thus leaving as
wide a space unincumbered in the middle part of
each deck, fore and aft, as our crowded situation
would admit.   Between these tiers of chests, &c.
and the sides of the ship, was the place where
the different messes assembled ; and some of the
messes were also separated from their neigbours
by a temporary partition of chests, &c.   Some
individuals of the different messes usually slept
on the chests, in order to preserve their contents
from being plundered during the night.

At night, the spaces in the middle of the deck
were much encumbered with hammocks ; but
these were always removed in the morning.

The prisoners, as before stated, were confined
on the two main decks below.   My usual place

of abode being in the Gun Room, on the centre
deck, I was never under the necessity of descending to the lower dungeon : and during my
confinement, I had no disposition to visit it.   It
was inhabited by the most wretched in appearance of all our miserable company.   From the
disgusting and squalid appearance of the groupes
which I saw ascending the stairs which led to it,
it must have been more dismal, if possible, than
that part of the hulk where I resided.   Its occupants appeared to be mostly foreigners, who had
seen and survived every variety of human suffering.   The faces of many of them were covered
with dirt and filth ; their long hair and beards
matted and foul : clothed in rags ; and with
scarcely a sufficient supply of these to cover
their disgusting bodies.   Many among them
possessed no clothing except the remnants of
those garments which they wore when first
brought on board ; and were unable to procure
even any materials for patching these together,
when they had been worn to tatters by constant
use ; and had this been in their power, they had
not the means of procuring a piece of thread, or

even a needle. Some, and indeed many of them, had not the means of procuring a razor or an ounce of soap.

Their beards were occasionally reduced by each other, with a pair of shears or scissors; but this operation, though conducive to cleanliness, was not productive of much improvement in their personal appearance. The skins of many of them were discolored by continual washing in salt water, added to the circumstance that it was impossible for them to wash their linen in any other manner, than by laying it on the deck, and stamping on it with their feet, after it had been immersed in salt water; their bodies remaining naked during the operation.

To men thus situated, everything like ordinary cleanliness was impossible. Much that was disgusting in their appearance undoubtedly originated from neglect, which long confinement had rendered habitual, until it created a confirmed indifference to personal appearance.

As soon as the gratings had been fastened over the hatchways for the night, we generally went to our sleeping places. It was, of course, always desirable to obtain a station as near as possible to the side of the ship; and, if practicable, in the immediate vicinity of one of the air-ports; as this not only afforded us a better air, but also rendered us less liable to be trodden upon by those who were moving about the decks during the night.

But silence was a stranger to our dark abode. There were continual noises during the night. The groans of the sick and the dying; the curses poured out by the weary and exhausted upon our inhuman keepers; the restlessness caused by the suffocating heat and the confined and poisoned air; mingled with the wild and incoherent ravings of delirium, were the sounds, which, every night, were raised around us, in all directions. Such was our ordinary situation; but at times, the consequences of our crowded condition were still more terrible, and proved fatal to many of our number in a single night.

But, strange as it may appear, notwithstanding all the maladies and sufferings which were there endured, I knew many who had been inmates of that abode for two years, who were apparently well. They had, as they expressed it, "been through the furnace, and become *seasoned.*" Most of these, however, were foreigners, who appeared to have abandoned all hope of ever being exchanged, and had become quite indifferent in regard to their place of abode.

But far different was the condition of that portion of our number who were natives of the Northern States. These formed by far the most numerous class of the prisoners. Most of these were young men, who had been induced by necessity or inclination to try the perils of the sea, and had, in many instances, been captured soon after leaving their homes, and during their first voyage. After they had been here immured, the sudden change in their situation was like a sentence of death. Many a one was crushed down beneath that sickness of the heart, so well described by the Poet, —

> ———— " Night and day,
> Brooding on what he had been, what he was ;
> ' Twas more than he could bear.   His longing fits
> Thickened upon him.   *His desire for Home
> Became a madness.*"

These poor creatures had, in many instances, been plundered of their wearing apparel by their captors. And here the dismal and disgusting objects by which they were surrounded; the vermin which infested them; their vile and loathsome food; and what, with *them*, was far from being the lightest of their trials, their ceaseless longing after their *homes* and the scenes to which they had been accustomed, — all combined to produce a wonderful effect upon them. Dejection and anguish were soon visible in their countenances. They became dismayed and terror stricken; and many of them absolutely died that most awful of all human deaths, the effects of *a broken heart*.

> " Denied the comforts of a dying bed,
>   With not a pillow to support the head ;
>   How could they else, but pine and grieve and sigh,
>   Detest that wretched life, and *wish* to die ? "

CHAPTER VII.

THE WORKING PARTY.

" No masts or sails these crowded ships adorn,
" Dismal to view, neglected and forlorn ;
" Here mighty ills oppress'd the imprison'd throng,
" Dull were our slumbers, and our nights were long —
" From morn to eve, along the decks we lay,
" Scorch'd into fevers by the solar ray."

FRENEAU.

A CUSTOM had long been established, that certain labour which it was necessary should be performed daily, should be done by a company, usually called the " Working Party." This consisted of about twenty able-bodied men, chosen from among the prisoners, and was commanded, in daily rotation, by those of our number who had formerly been officers of vessels. The commander of the party for the day bore

the title of *Boatswain*. The members of the
Working Party received, as a compensation for
their services, a full allowance of provisions, and
a half pint of rum each per day ; with the privilege of going on deck early in the morning, to
breathe the pure air. This privilege alone was
a sufficient compensation for all the duty which
was required of them.

Their routine of service was, to wash down
that part of the upper deck and gangways where
the prisoners were permitted to walk ; to spread
the awning ; and to hoist on board the wood,
water, and other supplies, from the boats in
which the same were brought along side the
ship.

When the prisoners ascended the upper deck
in the morning, if the day was fair, each carried
up his hammock and bedding ; which were all
placed upon the spar deck or booms. The
Working Party then took the sick and disabled
who remained below, and placed them in the
bunks prepared for them upon the centre deck ;
they then, if any of the prisoners had died during the night, carried up the dead bodies, and

laid them upon the booms.   After which, it was
their duty to wash down the main decks below;
during which operation the prisoners remained
upon the upper deck, except such as chose to go
below, and volunteer their services in the performance of this duty.

Around the railing of the hatchway leading
from the centre to the lower deck, were placed
a number of large tubs for the occasional use of
the prisoners during the night, and as general
receptacles of filth.   Although these were in-
dispensably necessary to us, yet they were
highly offensive.   Nevertheless, on account of
our crowded situation, many of the prisoners
were obliged to sleep in their immediate vicinity.
It was a part of the duty of the Working Party
to carry these tubs on deck, at the time when
the prisoners ascended in the morning; and
to return them between decks in the afternoon.

Our beds and clothing were kept on deck until it was nearly the hour when we were to be
ordered below for the night.   During this interval, the chests, &c. on the lower deck being

piled up, and the hammocks removed, the decks washed and cleared of all incumbrances except the poor wretches who lay in the bunks, it was quite refreshing, after the suffocating heat and foul vapours of the night, to walk between decks. There was then some circulation of air through the ship; and for a few hours, our existence was in some degree tolerable.

About two hours before sunset, the order was generally issued for the prisoners to carry their hammocks, &c. below. After this had been done, we were allowed either to retire between decks, or to remain above until sunset, according to our own pleasure. Every thing which we could do conducive to cleanliness having then been performed, if we ever felt anything like enjoyment in this wretched abode, it was during this brief interval, when we breathed the cool air of the approaching night, and felt the luxury of our evening pipe. But short indeed was this period of repose. The working party were soon ordered to carry the tubs below; and we prepared to descend to our gloomy and crowded dungeons. This was no sooner done, than the gratings were closed over the hatch-ways, the sentinels stationed, and we left to sicken and pine beneath our accumulated torments, with our guards above crying aloud, through the long night, " *All's well !* "

13

CHAPTER VIII.

THE HOSPITAL SHIPS AND NURSES.

" Thou ' SCORPION,' fatal to the crowded throng,
" Dire theme of horror and Plutonian song,
" Requir'st my lay.   Thy sultry decks I know,
" And all the torments that exist below."

    *   *   *   *

" The briny wave that Hudson's bosom fills,
" Drained through her bottom in a thousand rills.
" Rotten and old, replete with sighs and groans,
" Scarce on the waters she sustained her bones.
" Here, doomed to toil, or founder in the tide,
" At the moist pumps incessantly we plied.
" Here, doomed to starve, like famished dogs, we tore
" The scant allowance which our tyrants bore."

FRENEAU.

THE *Jersey* was used as a place of confinement for *seamen only*.   I never knew an instance of a soldier being sent on board her as a prisoner. During my confinement in the summer of 1782, the average number of prisoners on board the

Jersey was about ONE THOUSAND. They were composed of the crews of vessels of all nations with whom the English were then at war. By far the greater number, however, had been captured in American vessels.

The three Hospital Ships, *Scorpion*, *Strombolo*, and *Hunter*, were used for the reception of the sick from the principal hulk. The *Jersey* at length became so crowded, and the mortality on board her increased so rapidly, that sufficient room could not be found on board the Hospital Ships for their reception. Under these dreadful circumstances it was determined to prepare a part of the upper deck of the *Jersey* for the reception of the sick from between decks. Bunks were therefore erected on the after part of the upper deck, on the larboard side; where those who felt the symptoms of approaching sickness could lie down, in order to be found by the Nurses as soon as possible; and be thereby also prevented from being trampled upon by the other prisoners, to which they were continually liable while lying on the deck.

I have stated that the number of the Hospital

Ships was three. One of them, however, was used rather as a store-ship and depot for the medical department, and as a station for the Doctor's Mates and boats' crews attending the whole. This ship was, I think, the *Hunter*.

I never was on board either of the Hospital Ships; and could never learn many particulars in relation to the treatment of the sufferers on board them ; for but few ever returned from their recesses to the *Jersey*. I knew but three such instances during the whole period of my imprisonment. But I could form some idea of the interior of the Hospital Ships, from viewing their outward appearance, which was disgusting in the highest degree. Knowing, as we did, from whence their wretched inmates had been taken, the sight of these vessels was terrible to us, and their appearance more shocking than that of our own miserable hulk.

But whatever might be our sensations on viewing the Hospital Ships, they were, undoubtedly, in many respects, preferable to the *Jersey*. They were not so crowded, and of course afforded more room for breathing. They were

furnished with awnings, and provided with a
wind-sail to each hatchway, for the purpose of
conducting the fresh air between decks, where
the sick were placed. And, more than all, the
hatchways were left open during the night, as
our kind keepers were under no apprehensions
of danger from the feeble and helpless wretches
who were there deposited.

When communication between the ships was
required, or any thing wanted, it was made known
by signals, which were promptly attended to by
the boats from the *Hunter*. Our condition caused
our keepers much labour, and furnished employment, which to some of them was far from being
agreeable.

There were on board the *Jersey*, among the
prisoners, about half a dozen men, known by the
appellation of " *Nurses.*" I never learnt by
whom they were appointed, or whether they had
any regular appointment at all. But one fact I
well knew, — they were all thieves. They
were, however, sometimes useful in assisting the
sick to ascend from below to the gangway on
the upper deck, to be examined by the visiting

14

Surgeon, who attended from the *Hunter* every day (when the *weather* was good). If a sick man was pronounced by the Surgeon to be a proper subject for one of the Hospital Ships, he was forthwith put into the boat in waiting alongside; but not without the loss or detention of all his effects, if he had any, as these were at once taken into possession by the Nurses as their own property.

I will here relate an incident — not on account of its extreme aggravation, but because it occurred immediately under my own eye — which will show in some degree the kind of treatment which was given by these Nurses to the poor, weak, and dying men who were left to their care, and who were about to be transported to a hospital ship, and, in all probability, in a few hours, to the sand bank on the shore.

I had found Mr. Robert Carver, our Gunner while on board the *Chance*, sick in one of the bunks where those retired who wished to be removed. He was without a bed or pillow, and had put on all the wearing apparel which he possessed, wishing to preserve it, and being sensible of his situation. I found him sitting upright in the bunk, with his great coat on over the rest of his garments, and his hat between his knees. The weather was excessively hot, and in the place where he lay the heat was overpowering. I at once saw that he was delirious, — a sure presage that his end was near. I took off his great coat, and having folded and placed it under his head for a pillow, I laid him down upon it, and went immediately to prepare him some tea. I was absent but a few minutes, and on returning, met one of the thievish Nurses with Carver's great coat in his hand. On ordering him to return it, his only reply was, that it was a perquisite of the Nurses, and the only one they had; that the man was dying, and the garment could be of no further use to him.

I, however, took possession of the coat, and, on my liberation, returned it to the family of the owner. Mr. Carver soon after expired where he lay. We procured a blanket, in which we wrapped his body, which was thus prepared for interment. Others of the crew of the *Chance* had died previous to that time. Mr. Carver was a man of strong and robust constitution. Such men were subject to the most violent attacks of the fever, and were also its most certain victims.

I attach no blame to our keepers in regard to the thievish habits of the Nurses, over whom they had no control. I have merely related this incident for the purpose of more clearly showing to what a state of wretchedness we were reduced.

CHAPTER IX.

THE INTERMENT OF THE DEAD.

" By feeble hands their shallow graves were made ;
" No stone, memorial, o'er their corpses laid.
" In barren sands, and far from home, they lie,
" No friend to shed a tear when passing by ;
" O'er the mean tombs, insulting foemen tread,
" Spurn at the sand, and curse the rebel dead.''

FRENEAU.

IT has already been mentioned that one of
the duties of the Working Party was, on each
morning, to place the sick in the bunks, and if
any of the prisoners had died during the night,
to carry the dead bodies to the upper deck,
where they were laid upon the gratings. Any
prisoner who could procure and chose to furnish
a blanket, was allowed to sew it around the remains of his deceased companions.

15

The signal being made, a boat was soon seen approaching from the *Hunter*; and if there were any dead on board the other ships, the boat received them on her way to the *Jersey*.

The corpse was laid upon a board, to which some ropes were attached as straps; as it was often the case that bodies were sent on shore for interment before they had become sufficiently cold and stiff to be lowered into the boat by a single strap. Thus prepared, a tackle was attached to the board, and the remains of the sufferer were hoisted over the side of the ship into the boat, without further ceremony. If several bodies were waiting for interment, but one of them was lowered into the boat at a time, for the sake of decency. The prisoners were always very anxious to be engaged in the duty of interment; not so much from a feeling of humanity, or from a wish of paying respect to the remains of the dead (for to these feelings they had almost become strangers), as from the desire of once more placing their feet upon the land, if but for a few minutes. A sufficient number of the prisoners having received permission to assist in this duty, they entered the boat, accompanied by a guard of soldiers, and put off from the ship.

I obtained leave to assist in the burial of the body of Mr. Carver, whose death was mentioned in the preceding Chapter. As this was done in the ordinary mode, a relation of the circumstances attending it will afford a correct idea of the general method of interment.

After landing at a low wharf which had been built from the shore, we first went to a small hut, which stood near the wharf, and was used as a place of deposit for the hand-barrows and shovels provided for these occasions. Having placed the corpses on the hand-barrows, and received our hoes and shovels, we proceeded to the side of the bank near the Wallabout. Here a vacant space having been selected, we were directed to dig a trench in the sand, of a proper length for the reception of the bodies. We continued our labour until our guards considered that a sufficient space had been excavated. The corpses were then laid into the trench, without ceremony, and we threw the sand over them.

The whole appeared to produce no more effect upon our guards, than if we were burying the bodies of dead animals instead of men. They scarcely allowed us time to look about us; for no sooner had we heaped the earth above the trench, than the order was given to march. But a single glance was sufficient to show us parts of many bodies which were exposed to view, although they had probably been placed there, with the same mockery of interment, but a few days before.

Having thus performed, as well as we were permitted to do it, the last duty to the dead, and the guards having stationed themselves on each side of us, we began reluctantly to retrace our steps to the boat. We had enjoyed the pleasure of breathing, for a few moments, the air of our native soil; and the thought of returning to the crowded prison-ship was terrible in the extreme. As we passed by the water's side, we implored our guards to allow us to bathe, or even to wash ourselves for a few minutes; but this was refused us.

I was the only prisoner of our party who wore

a pair of shoes, and well recollect the circumstance, that I took them from my feet for the pleasure of feeling the earth, or rather the sand, as I went along. It was a high gratification to us to bury our feet in the sand, and to shove them through it, as we passed on our way. We went by a small patch of turf, some pieces of which we tore up from the earth, and obtained permission to carry them on board, for our comrades to smell them. Circumstances like these may appear trifling to the careless reader ; but let him be assured that they were far from being trifles to men situated as we had been. The inflictions which we had endured ; the duty which we had just performed ; the feeling that we must in a few minutes re-enter our place of suffering, from which, in all probability, we should never return alive, — all tended to render every thing connected with the firm land beneath, and the sweet air above us, objects of deep and thrilling interest.

Having arrived at the hut, we there deposited our implements, and walked to the landing place, where we prevailed on our guards, who were

16

Hessians, to allow us the gratification of remaining nearly half an hour, before we re-entered the boat.

Near us stood a house, occupied by a miller; and we had been told that a tide-mill, which he attended, was in its immediate vicinity, as a landing place for which, the wharf where we stood had been erected. It would have afforded me a high degree of pleasure to have been permitted to enter this dwelling, the probable abode of harmony and peace. It was designated by the prisoners by the appellation of the " Old Dutchman's; " and its very walls were viewed by us with feelings of veneration, as we had been told that the amiable daughter of its owner had kept a regular account of the number of bodies which had been brought on shore for interment from the *Jersey* and the Hospital Ships. This could easily be done in the house, as its windows commanded a fair view of the landing place. We were not, however, gratified on this occasion, either by the sight of herself, or of any other inmate of the house.

Sadly did we approach and re-enter our foul

and disgusting place of confinement. The pieces of turf which we carried on board were sought for by our fellow-prisoners with the greatest avidity : every fragment being passed by them from hand to hand, and its smell inhaled, as if it had been a fragrant rose.

CHAPTER X.

THE CREW OF " THE CHANCE."

> ———— " At dead of night,
> " In sullen silence, stalks forth Pestilence :
> " Contagion, close behind, taints all her steps
> " With poisonous dew ; no smiting hand is seen ;
> " No sound is heard ; but soon her secret path
> " Is marked with desolation ; — heaps on heaps,
> " Promiscuous drop.   No friend, no refuge near :
> " All, all is false and treacherous around ;
> " All that they touch, or taste, or breathe, is death."

*   *   *   *   *

> " Yet, still they breathe destruction ; still go on,
> " Inhumanly ingenious, to find out
> " New pains for life, new terrors for the grave ;
> " Artificers of death ! "   PORTEUS.

My visit to the shore, as described in the last chapter, was the first one which I had been permitted to make.   I had then been a prisoner for several weeks, and my situation had become, in some degree, familiar; but my visit to the land caused me to feel the extent of my wretchedness, and to view my condition with feelings of greater abhorrence, and even of despair.

I have already observed that Mr. Carver was not the first victim among the crew of the *Chance*. The first individual was a lad named Palmer, about twelve years of age, the youngest of our crew. While on board the *Chance* he was a waiter to the officers, and he continued in that duty after we were placed on board the *Jersey*. He had, with many others of our crew, been inoculated for the small pox, immediately after our arrival on board. The usual symptoms appeared at the proper time, and we supposed the appearances of his disorder to be favourable; but these soon changed, and the yellow hue of his features declared the approach of death. He became delirious, and died during the succeeding night. He was a member of the same mess with myself, and had always looked up to me as a protector, and particularly so during his sickness. That night was truly a wretched one to me; for I spent almost the whole of it in perfect dark-

17

ness, holding him during his convulsions; and it was heart-rending to hear the screams of the dying boy, while calling and imploring, in his delirium, for the assistance of his mother and other persons of his family. For a long time, all persuasion or argument was useless to silence his groans and supplications. But exhausted nature at length sunk under its agonies; his screams became less piercing, and his struggles less violent. In the midnight gloom of our dungeon, I could not see him die; but knew, by placing my hand over his mouth, that his breathings were becoming shorter; and thus felt the last breath as it quit his frame. The first glimmer of morning light through the iron grate, fell upon his pallid and lifeless corpse.

I had done every thing in my power for this poor boy during his sickness, and could render him but one more kind office. I assisted in sewing a blanket round his body, which was, with those of the others who had died during the night, conveyed upon deck in the morning, to be, at the usual hour, hurried to the bank at the Wallabout. I regretted that I could not assist at his interment; but this was impossible, as I was then suffering with the small pox myself; neither am I certain that permission would have been granted me if I had sought it. Our keepers seemed to have no idea that the prisoners could feel any regard for each other; but appeared to think us as cold-hearted as themselves. If any thing like sympathy was ever shewn us by any of them, it was done by the Hessians. In fact, the prisoners had lost almost every feeling of humanity for each other; and being able to reciprocate but few offices of kindness, their feelings had become withered, and self-preservation appeared to be their only wish.

The next deaths among our own crew were those of James Mitchell, and his son-in-law, Thomas Sturmey. It is a singular fact that both of these men died at the same time. I did not even know that either of them had been sick; and my first intimation of the fact was when I was told that their bodies were lying on the grating, on the upper deck. I there found them lying in the same clothes in which they had died. We procured a couple of blankets, and placed

them around the bodies, previous to their interment.   I applied for permission to accompany
their remains to the land, and to assist in their
burial; but this was denied me.   I, however,
watched their progress to the shore, and saw
them deposited in the bank.   Mr. Mitchell was
generally known among his fellow-citizens of
Providence; and there are many now living who
well recollect him.

It will, at first, appear almost incredible, that
my former companions, my friends, and fellow-
townsmen, could be thus sick and dying, so near
me, and I remain in profound ignorance of the
fact.   But such was in reality our situation in
this little world of concentrated misery.   We
were separated and scattered over the different
parts of the crowded hulk, and mingled with the
great mass of the prisoners; and, sometimes
meeting each other, among the multitude, we
would, on enquiring respecting the fate of an old
comrade, receive the appalling information that
he had either been attacked by sickness and removed to one of the Hospital Ships, or had died,
and gone to his last home under the bank of the
Wallabout.

CHAPTER XI.

THE MARINE GUARD.

" Remembrance shudders at this scene of fears, —
" Still in my view some tyrant chief appears,
" Some base-born Hessian slave walks threatening by,
" Some servile Scot, with murder in his eye,
" Still haunts my sight, as vainly they bemoan
" *Rebellions* manag'd so unlike *their own*."

      *   *   *   *   *

" No waters laded from the bubbling spring,
" To these dire ships these little tyrants bring, —
" No drop was granted to the midnight prayer,
" To *Rebels* in these regions of despair !
" The loathsome cask a deadly dose contains ;
" Its poison circling through the languid veins."

FRENEAU.

IN addition to the regular officers and seamen
of the *Jersey*, there were stationed on board
about a dozen old invalid marines ; but our actual guard was composed of soldiers from the

18

different regiments quartered on Long Island.
The number usually on duty on board was about
thirty. Each week they were relieved by a fresh
party. They were English, Hessians, and Refugees. We always preferred the Hessians, from
whom we received better treatment than from
the others. As to the English, we did not complain, being aware that they merely obeyed their
orders in regard to us ; but the Refugees, or Royalists, as they termed themselves, were viewed
by us with scorn and hatred. I do not recollect, however, that a guard of these miscre-
ants was placed over us more than three times,
during which their presence occasioned much
tumult and confusion ; for the prisoners could
not endure the sight of these men, and occasionally assailed them with abusive language ; while
they, in return, treated us with all the severity
in their power.

We dared not approach near them for fear of
their bayonets: and of course could not pass along
the gangways where they were stationed ; but
were obliged to crawl along upon the booms, in
order to get fore and aft, or to go up or down

the hatchways. They never answered any of
our remarks respecting them; but would merely
point to their uniforms, as if saying, We are
clothed by our Sovereign, while you are naked.
They were as much gratified at the idea of leaving us, as we were at seeing them depart. Many
provoking gestures were made by the prisoners
as they left the ship, and our curses followed
them as far as we could make ourselves heard.

A regiment of Refugees, with a green uni-
form, was then quartered at Brooklyn. We
were invited to join this Royal Band, and to par-
take of his Majesty's pardon and bounty. But
the prisoners, in the midst of their unbounded
suffering, of their dreadful privation and consum-
ing anguish, spurned the insulting offer. They
preferred to linger and to die, rather than desert
their country's cause. During the whole period
of my confinement, I never knew a single instance of enlistment from among the prisoners of
the *Jersey*.

The only duty, to my knowledge, ever performed by the old marines, was to guard the
water butt, near which one of them was stationed

with a drawn cutlass. They were ordered to
allow no prisoner to carry away more than one
pint of water at once; but we were allowed to
drink at the butt as much as we pleased; for
which purpose two or three copper ladles were
chained to the cask. Having been long on
board, and regular in the performance of this
duty, they had become familiar with the faces of
the prisoners; and could thereby, in many instances, detect the frauds which we practised
upon them in order to obtain more fresh water
for our cooking than was allowed us by the regulations of the ship. Over the water the soldiers
had no control.

The daily consumption of water on board was
at least equal to seven hundred gallons. I know
not whence it was brought, but presume it was
from Brooklyn. One large gondola, or boat,
was kept in constant employment to furnish the
necessary supply.

So much of the water as was not required on
deck for immediate use, was conducted into butts
placed in the lower hold of the hulk, through a
leathern hose, passing through her side, near the

bends. To this water we had recourse when we could procure no other.

When water in any degree fit for use was brought on board, it is impossible to describe the struggle which ensued in consequence of our haste and exertions to procure a draught of it. The best which was ever afforded us was very brackish; but that from the ship's hold was nauseous in the highest degree. This must be evident when the fact is stated, that the butts for receiving it had never been cleaned since they were placed in the hold. The quantity of foul sediment which they contained was therefore very great, and was disturbed and mixed with the water, as often as a new supply was poured into them; thereby rendering their whole contents a substance of the most disgusting and poisonous nature. I have not the least doubt that the use of this vile compound caused the death of hundreds of the prisoners, when, to allay their tormenting thirst, they were driven by desperation to drink this liquid poison, and to abide the consequences.

CHAPTER XII.

"DAME GRANT" AND HER BOAT.

> " At *Brooklyn Wharf*, in travelling trim,
> " Young Charon's boat receives her store ;
> " Across the wavy waste they skim,
> " She at the helm, and he, the oar.
>
> " The market done, her cash secure,
> " She homeward takes her wonted way ;
> " The painted chest, behind the door,
> " Receives the gainings of the day."
>
> THE MARKET GIRL.

ONE indulgence was allowed us by our keepers ; if indulgence it may be called. They had
given permission for a boat to come alongside
the ship with a supply of a few necessary articles, to be sold to such of the prisoners as possessed the means of paying for them.

This trade was carried on by a very corpulent old woman, known among the prisoners by the name of " DAME GRANT." Her visits, which were made on every other day, were of much benefit to us, and I presume a source of profit to herself. She brought us soft bread and fruit, with various other articles, such as sugar, tea, &c. all of which she previously put up into small paper parcels, from one ounce to a pound in weight, with the price affixed to each, from which she would never deviate. The bulk of the old lady completely filled the stern sheets of the boat; where she sat, with her box of goods before her, from which she supplied us very expeditiously. Her boat was rowed by two boys, who delivered to us the articles we had purchased; the price of which we were required first to put into their hands.

When our guard was not composed of Refugees, we were usually permitted to descend to the foot of the accommodation ladder, in order to select from the boat such articles as we wished. While standing there, it was distressing to see the faces of hundreds of half famished wretches, looking over the side of the ship into the boat, without the means of purchasing the most trifling article before their sight; not even so much as a morsel of wholesome bread. None of us possessed the means of generosity, nor had any power to afford them relief. Whenever I bought any articles from the boat, I never enjoyed them; for it was impossible to do so in the presence of so many needy wretches, eagerly gazing at my purchase, and almost dying for want of it.

We frequently furnished Dame Grant with a memorandum of such articles as we wished her to procure for us, such as pipes, tobacco, needles, thread, and combs. These she always faithfully procured and brought to us; never omitting the assurance that she afforded them exactly *at cost*.

Her arrival was always a subject of interest to us; but at length she did not make her appearance for several days; and her approach was awaited in extreme anxiety. But, alas! we were no longer to enjoy this little gratification. Her traffic was ended. She had taken the fever from the hulk, and died, — if not in the flower of her youth, at least in the midst of her use-fulness, leaving a void which was never after-wards filled up.

20

CHAPTER XIII.

OUR SUPPLIES.

" On the hard floors, these wasted objects laid,
" There tossed and tumbled in the dismal shade.
" There no soft voice their bitter fate bemoaned,
" And death trod stately while his victims groaned."

FRENEAU.

AFTER the death of Dame Grant, we were under the necessity of purchasing from the Sutler such small supplies as we needed. This man was one of the Mates of the ship, and occupied one of the apartments under the quarter deck, through the bulk head of which an opening had been cut, from which he delivered his goods. He here kept for sale a variety of articles, among which was usually a supply of ardent spirits, which was not allowed to be brought alongside the ship for sale. It could therefore only be procured from the Sutler, whose price was two dollars for a gallon. Except in relation to this article, no regular price was fixed for what he sold us. We were first obliged to hand him the money, and he then gave us such a quantity as he pleased of the article which we needed; there was, on our part, no bargain to be made. But, to be supplied even in this manner, was, to those of us who had means of payment, a great convenience.

But how different was our condition from that of our countrymen who were sent prisoners to England, during the same period. They were also in confinement, it is true, but it was in prisons which were palaces in comparison with the foul and putrid dungeons into which we were crowded. They were furnished with sweet and wholesome provisions, and with pure and good water for every necessary purpose. They could easily procure vegetables, and every other supply conducive to their comfort. An Agent was appointed to supply them with clothing and to attend to their complaints. They had a sufficient space for exercise and manly recreation during the day, and the privilege of using lights by night. They were not so crowded together as to be thereby rendered the almost certain victims of disease and death. They received donations from the charitable and the well disposed. Such was *their* situation, in a foreign country, — in the land of our enemies. What a contrast does this present to the picture I have attempted to give of *our* condition, while confined on our own waters, and in sight of our own shore! Our own people afforded us no relief. Oh, my Country! why were we thus neglected in this our hour of misery, — why was not a little food and raiment given to the dying martyrs of thy cause?

Although the supplies which some of us were enabled to procure from the Sutler were highly conducive to our comfort, yet one most necessary article neither himself nor any other person could furnish us. This was wood for our daily cooking; to procure a sufficient quantity of which, was to us a source of continual trouble and anxiety. The cooks would indeed steal small quantities, and sell them to us, at the hazard of certain punishment if detected ; but it was not in their power to embezzle a sufficient quantity to meet our daily necessities. As the disgust of swallowing any food which had been cooked in the Great Copper was universal, each prisoner used every exertion to procure as much wood as possible, for the private cooking of his own mess.

During my excursion to the shore, to assist in the interment of Mr. Carver, it was my good fortune to find a hogshead stave floating in the water. This was truly a prize. I conveyed the treasure on board ; and in the economical manner in which it was used, it furnished the mess to which I belonged with a supply of fuel for a considerable time.

I was also truly fortunate on another occasion. I had, one day, command of the Working Party, which was then employed in taking on board a sloop load of wood for the ship's use. This was carefully conveyed below, under a guard, to prevent embezzlement. I nevertheless found means, with the assistance of my associates, to convey a cleft of it into the Gun Room, where it was immediately secreted. Our mess was thereby supplied with a sufficient quantity for a long time; and its members were considered by far the most wealthy persons in all this republic of misery. We had enough for our own use, and were enabled occasionally to supply our neighbours with a few splinters.

Our mode of preparing the wood for use was to cut it with a jack knife, into pieces about four inches long. This labour occupied much of our time, and was performed by the different members of the mess, in rotation; which employment was to us a source of no little pleasure.

After a sufficient quantity had thus been prepared for the next day's use, it was deposited in the chest. The main stock was guarded, by day and night, with the most scrupulous and anxious care. We kept it at night within our own enclosure; and by day it was always watched by some one of its proprietors. So highly did we value it, that we went into mathematical calculations to ascertain how long it would supply us, if a given quantity was each day consumed.

It may be thought that this subject is not of sufficient importance to be so long dwelt upon. But things which are usually of trifling worth may, at times, become objects of the greatest consequence. Men may be placed in situations where the flint is of more value than the diamond.

CHAPTER XIV.

OUR BY-LAWS.

" What though the sun, in his meridian blaze,
" Dart on their naked limbs his scorching rays ;
" Still, of etherial temper are their souls,
" And in their veins the tide of honour rolls."

DAY.

SOON after the *Jersey* was first used as a place
of confinement, a code of By-Laws had been
established by the prisoners, for their own regu-
lation and government, to which a willing sub-
mission was paid, so far as circumstances would
permit. I much regret my inability to give these
rules verbatim ; but I cannot at this distant period
of time recollect them with a sufficient degree
of distinctness. They were chiefly directed to
the preservation of personal cleanliness, and the
prevention of immorality. For a refusal to com-

ply with any one of them, the refractory prisoner was subject to a stated punishment. It is an astonishing fact that any rules thus made should have so long existed and been enforced among a multitude of men situated as we were ; so numerous, and composed of individuals of that class of human beings who are not easily controlled, and usually not the most ardent supporters of good order. There were many foreigners among our number, over whom we had no control, except so far as they chose voluntarily to comply with our regulations ; which they cheerfully did, in almost every instance, so far as their condition would allow.

Among our Rules were the following : That personal cleanliness should be preserved, as far as was practicable ; that profane language should be avoided ; that drunkenness should not be allowed ; that theft should be severely punished ; and that no smoking should be permitted between decks, by day or night, on account of the annoyance which it caused to the sick.

A due observance of the Sabbath was also strongly enjoined ; and it was recommended to every individual to appear cleanly shaved on Sunday morning, and to refrain from all recreation during the day. This rule was particularly recommended to the attention of the officers, and the remainder of the prisoners were desired to follow their example.

Our By-Laws were occasionally read to the assembled prisoners, and always whenever any prisoner was to be punished for their violation. Theft or fraud upon the allowance of a fellow-prisoner was always punished, and the infliction was always approved by the whole company. On these occasions the oldest officer among the prisoners presided as Judge.

It required much exertion for many of us to comply with the law prohibiting smoking between decks. Being myself much addicted to the habit of smoking, it would have been a great privilege to have enjoyed the liberty of thus indulging it, particularly during the night, while sitting by one of the air ports; but as this was entirely inadmissible, I of course submitted to the prohibition.

Many of us waited in great anxiety for the

moment when we could ascend to the upper
deck, and enjoy the gratification of our favourite
habit. The practice had indeed become universal among the prisoners, at least as many of them
as had the means of procuring tobacco. We
were allowed no means of striking fire, and were
obliged to procure it from the Cook employed
for the ship's officers, through a small window
in the bulk head, near the camboose. After one
had thus procured fire, the rest were also soon
supplied, and our pipes were all in full operation
in the course of a few minutes. The smoke
which rose around us appeared to purify the
pestilential air by which we were surrounded;
and I attributed the preservation of my health in
a great degree to the exercise of this habit. Our
greatest difficulty was to procure tobacco. This,
to some of the prisoners, was impossible; and it
must have been an aggravation to their sufferings to see us apparently puffing away our sor-
rows, while they had no means of procuring the
enjoyment of a similar gratification.

We dared not often apply at this Cook's camboose for fire, as the surly wretch would not

willingly repeat the supply. One morning I went to the window of his den, and requested leave to light my pipe; and the miscreant, without making any reply, threw a shovel full of burning cinders in my face. I was almost blinded by the pain, and several days elapsed before I fully regained my sight. My feelings on this occasion may be imagined; but redress was impossible, as we were allowed no mode of even seeking it. I mention this occurrence to show to what a wretched state we were reduced, when thus exposed to the wanton and vexatious insults, the petty and disgusting tyranny of all those wretches, from the Commissary to the Cook and the Cook's scullion. This wanton act of that inhuman monster would not probably have been justified by the Captain, had it come to his knowledge; but it was wholly out of our power to devise means whereby to convey any complaint to him. Had the means been allowed us of making known our grievances, many of these brutal aggressions would probably have been punished, and we should have been saved from the endurance of a great number of petty, but unceasing insults.

CHAPTER XV.

OUR ORATOR.

——— " Stranger Youth,
" So noble and so mild is thy demeanour,
" So gentle and so patient ; such the air
" Of candour and of courage which adorns
" Thy manly features, thou hast won my love."

H. MOORE.

DURING the period of my confinement, the *Jersey* was never visited by any regular clergy-man, nor was Divine service ever performed on board. And among the whole multitude of the prisoners, there was but one individual who ever attempted to deliver a set speech, or to exhort his fellow-sufferers.

This individual was a young man named Cooper, whose station in life was apparently that

23

of a common sailor.   He was a man of eccentric character, but evidently possessed talents of a very high order.   His manners were pleasing, and he had every appearance of having received an excellent education.   He was a Virginian; but I never learnt the exact place of his nativity. He told us that he had been a very unmanageable youth, and that he had left his family contrary to their wishes and advice; that he had often been assured by them that the old *Jersey* would bring him up at last, and the Wallabout be his place of burial.   " The first of these predictions," said he, " has been verified;   and I care not how soon the second proves equally true, for I am prepared for the event.   Death, for me, has lost its terrors, for with them I have been too long familiar."

On several Sunday mornings Cooper harangued the prisoners in a very forcible yet pleasing manner, which, together with his language, made a lasting impression upon my memory. On one of these occasions, having mounted a temporary elevation on the spar deck, he, in an audible voice, requested the attention of the prisoners, who having immediately gathered round him in silence, he commenced his discourse.

He began by saying that he hoped no one would suppose he had taken that station by way of derision or mockery of that holy day, for that such was not his object ; on the contrary, he was pleased to find that the good regulations established by the former prisoners obliged us to refrain even from recreation on the Sabbath ; that his object, however, was not to preach to us, nor to discourse upon any sacred subject. He wished to read us our By-Laws, a copy of which he held in his hand ; the framers of which were then in all probability sleeping in death, beneath the sand of the shore before our eyes. That these laws had been framed in wisdom, and were well fitted to preserve order and decorum in a community like ours ; that his present object was to impress upon our minds the absolute necessity of a strict adherence to those wholesome regulations ; that he should briefly comment upon each article, which might be thus considered as the particular text of that part of his discourse.

He proceeded to point out the extreme neces-

sity of a full observance of these Rules of Conduct ; and pourtrayed the evil consequences
which would inevitably result to us, if we neglected or suffered them to fall into disuse. He
enforced the necessity of our unremitted attention to personal cleanliness, and to the duties of
morality ; he dwelt on the degradation and sin of
drunkenness; described the meanness and atrocity
of theft; and the high degree of caution against
temptation necessary for men who were perhaps
standing on the very brink of the grave; and
added that, in his opinion, even sailors might as
well refrain from profane language while they
were actually suffering in Purgatory.

He said that our present torments in that
abode of misery were a proper retribution for
our former sins and transgressions; that Satan
had been permitted to send out his messengers
and inferior demons in every direction to collect
us together; and that among the most active of
these infernal agents was *David Sproat*, *Commissary of Prisoners*.

He then made some just and suitable observa-
tions on the fortitude with which we had sus-

tained the weight of our accumulated miseries;
of our firmness in refusing to accept the bribes
of our invaders and desert the banners of our
country. During this part of his discourse, the
sentinels on the gangways occasionally stopped
and listened attentively. We much feared, that
by some imprudent remark, he might expose
himself to their resentment; and cautioned him
not to proceed too far. He replied that our
keepers could do nothing more, unless they
should put him to the torture, and that he should
proceed.

He touched on the fact that no clergyman had
ever visited us; that this was probably owing to
the fear of contagion; but it was much to be regretted that no one had ever come to afford a
ray of hope, or to administer the Word of Life
in that terrific abode; that if any Minister of the
Gospel desired to do so, there could be no ob-
stacle in the way; for that even David Sproat
himself, bad as he was, would not dare to
oppose it.

He closed with a merited tribute to the memory of those of our fellow-sufferers who had

already paid the debt of nature. "The time," said he, "will come, when their bones will be collected; when their rites of sepulture will be performed; and a monument erected over the remains of those who have here suffered, the victims of barbarity, and died in vindication of the rights of Man."

I have myself lived to see his predictions verified. Those bones have been collected; those rites have been performed; that monument has been raised.

The remarks of our Orator were well adapted to our situation, and produced much effect upon the prisoners, who at length began to accost him as "Elder," or "Parson Cooper." But this he would not allow; and told us, if we would insist on giving him a title, we might call him "Doctor;" by which name he was ever afterwards saluted, so long as he remained among us.

He had been a prisoner for about the period of three months, when, one day, the Commissary of Prisoners came on board, accompanied by a stranger, and enquired for Cooper; who, having made his appearance, a letter was put into his

hand, which he perused, and immediately afterwards left the ship, without even going below
for his clothing.   While in the boat, he waved
his hand, and bid us be of good cheer.   We
could only return a mute farewell ; and in a few
moments the boat had left the ship, and was on
its way to New York.

Thus we lost our Orator, for whom I had a
very high regard at the time, and whose character and manners have, ever since, been to me a
subject of pleasing recollection.

Various were the conjectures which the sudden manner of his departure caused on board.
Some asserted that poor Cooper had drawn upon
himself the vengeance of old Sproat, and that he
had been carried on shore to be punished.   No
certain information was ever received respecting
him ; but I have always thought that he was a
member of some highly influential and respect-
able family, and that his release had been effected
through the agency of his friends.   This was
often done by the influence of the Royalists or
Refugees in New York, who were sometimes
the connexions or personal friends of those who

applied for their assistance in procuring the liberation of a son or a brother from captivity. Such kind offices were thus frequently rendered to those who had chosen opposite sides in the great revolutionary contest ; and to whom, though directly opposed to themselves in political proceedings, they were willing to render every personal service in their power.

CHAPTER XVI.

THE FOURTH OF JULY.

" Black as the clouds that shade St. Kilda's shore,
" Wild as the winds that round her mountains roar,
" At every post some surly vagrant stands,
" Cull'd from the English or the Scottish bands.
" Dispensing death, triumphantly they stand ;
" Their muskets ready to obey command,
" Wounds are their sport, as ruin is their aim ;
" On their dark souls compassion has no claim ;
" And discord only can their spirits please :
" Such were our tyrants ; only such as these."

FRENEAU.

A FEW days before the fourth of July, we had made such preparations as our circumstances would admit for an observance of the anniversary of American Independence. We had procured some supplies wherewith to make ourselves merry on the occasion ; and intended to

25

spend the day in such innocent pastime and amusement as our situation would afford ; not dreaming that our proceedings would give umbrage to our keepers, as it was far from our intention to trouble or insult them. We thought, that although prisoners, we had a right, on that day at least, to sing and be merry. As soon as we were permitted to go on deck in the morning, thirteen little national flags were displayed in a row upon the booms. We were soon ordered by the guard to take them away ; and as we neglected to obey the command, they triumphantly demolished and trampled them under foot.

Unfortunately for us, our guards at that time were Scotchmen, who, next to the Refugees, were the objects of our greatest hatred ; but their destruction of our flags was merely viewed in silence, with the contempt which it merited.

During the time we remained on deck, several patriotic songs were sung, and choruses were repeated ; but not a word was intentionally spoken to give offence to our guards. They were, nevertheless, evidently dissatisfied with our proceed-

ings, as will soon appear. Their moroseness
was a prelude to what was to follow. We were
in a short time forbidden to pass along the common gangways, and every attempt to do so was
repelled by the bayonet. Although thus incom-
moded, our mirth still continued. Songs were
still sung, accompanied with occasional cheers.
Things thus proceeded until about four o'clock,
when the guards were turned out, and we received orders to descend between decks, where
we were immediately driven, at the point of the
bayonet.

After being thus sent below in the greatest
confusion, at that early and unusual hour, and
having heard the gratings closed and fastened
above us, we supposed that the barbarous resentment of our guards was fully satisfied; but we
were mistaken, for they had further vengeance
in store, and merely waited for an opportunity to
make us feel its weight.

The prisoners continued their singing between
decks, and were of course more noisy than usual,
but forbore, even under their existing tempta-
tions, to utter any insulting or aggravating ex-

pressions.   At least, I heard nothing of the kind, unless our patriotic songs could be so construed.

In the course of the evening we were ordered to desist from making any further noise.   This order not being fully complied with, at about nine o'clock the gratings were removed, and the guards descended among us, with lanterns and drawn cutlasses in their hands.   The poor, help-less prisoners retreated from the hatchways, as far as their crowded situation would permit ; while their cowardly assailants followed as far as they dared, cutting and wounding every one within their reach ; and then ascended to the upper deck, exulting in the gratification of their revenge.

Many of the prisoners were wounded ; but, from the total darkness, neither their number nor their situation could be ascertained ; and, if this had been possible, it was not in the power of their companions to afford them the least relief. During the whole of that tragical night, their groans and lamentations were dreadful in the extreme.   Being in the Gun Room, I was at some distance from the immediate scene of this

bloody outrage ; but the distance was by no
means far enough to prevent my hearing their
continual cries, from the extremity of pain, their
applications for assistance, and their curses upon
the heads of their brutal assailants.

It had been the usual custom for each prisoner to
carry below, when he descended at sunset, a pint
of water, to quench his thirst during the night.
But on this occasion we had thus been driven to
our dungeons, three hours before the setting of
the sun, and without our usual supply of water.

Of this night I cannot describe the horrors.
The day had been very sultry, and the heat was
extreme throughout the ship. The unusual number of hours during which we had been crowded
together between decks, the foul atmosphere and
sickening heat, the additional excitement and
restlessness caused by the wanton attack which
had been made ; above all, the want of water,
not a drop of which could we obtain during the
whole night to cool our parched tongues ; the
imprecations of those who were half-distracted

of the dying, together formed a combination of horrors which no pen can describe.

In the agonies of their suffering, the prisoners invited, and even challenged, their inhuman guards to descend once more among them; but this they were prudent enough not to attempt.

Their cries and supplications for water were terrible, and were, of themselves, sufficient to render sleep impossible. Oppressed with the heat, I found my way to the grating of the main hatchway, where on former nights I had frequently passed some time, for the benefit of the little current of air which circulated through the bars. I obtained a place on the larboard side of the hatchway, where I stood facing the East, and endeavoured, as much as possible, to draw my attention from the terrific sounds below me, by watching through the grating the progress of the stars. I there spent hour after hour in following with my eye the motion of a particular star, as it rose and ascended, until it passed over beyond my sight.

How I longed for the day to dawn! At length the morning light began to appear; but still our torments were increasing every moment. As the usual hour for us to ascend to the upper deck approached, the Working Party were mustered near the hatchway, and we were all anxiously waiting for the opportunity to cool our weary frames, to breathe for a while the pure air, and, above all, to procure water to quench our intolerable thirst. The time arrived, but still the gratings were not removed. Hour after hour passed on, and still we were not released. Our minds were at length seized with the horrible suspicion that our tyrants had determined to make a finishing stroke of their cruelty, and rid themselves of us altogether.

It was not until ten o'clock in the forenoon that the gratings were at length removed. We hurried on deck, and thronged to the water cask, which was completely exhausted before our thirst was allayed. So great was the struggle around the cask, that the guards were again turned out to disperse the crowd.

In a few hours, however, we received a new supply of water; but it seemed impossible to allay our thirst, and the applications at the cask were incessant until sunset.

Our rations were delivered to us; but, of course, not until long after the usual hour. During the whole day, however, no fire was kindled for cooking in the Galley. All the food which we consumed that day we were obliged to swallow raw. Everything, indeed, had been entirely deranged by the events of the past night, and several days elapsed before order was restored. This was at length obtained by a change of the guard, who, to our great joy, were relieved by a party of Hessians.

The average number who died on board, during the period of twenty-four hours, was about five; but on the morning of the fifth of July, eight or ten corpses were found below. Many had been badly wounded, to whom, in the total darkness of the night, it was impossible for their companions to render any assistance; and even during the next day they received no attention, except that which was afforded by their fellow-prisoners, who had nothing to administer to their comfort, — not even bandages for their wounds.

I was not personally acquainted with any of those who died or were wounded on that night.

No equal number had ever died in the same period of time during my confinement. This unusual mortality was of course caused by the increased sufferings of the night.

Since that time, I have often, while standing on the deck of a good ship under my command, and viewing the rising stars, thought upon the terrors of that night when I stood watching their progress through the gratings of the old *Jersey*. And when I now contrast my former wretchedness with my present situation, in the full enjoyment of liberty, health, and every earthly comfort, I cannot but muse upon the contrast, and bless the great and good Being from whom my comforts have been derived. I do not now regret my captivity nor my sufferings; for the recollection of them has ever taught me how to enjoy my after life, with a greater degree of contentment than I should perhaps have otherwise ever experienced.

CHAPTER XVII.

AN ATTEMPT TO ESCAPE.

" Better the greedy wave should swallow all,
" Better to meet the death-conducting ball,
" Better to sleep on ocean's oozy bed,
" At once destroy'd and number'd with the dead ;
" Than thus to perish in the face of day,
" Where twice ten thousand deaths one death delay."

FRENEAU.

IT had been some time in contemplation, among
a few of the inmates of the Gun Room, to make
a desperate attempt to escape, by cutting a hole
through the stern or counter of the ship. In
order that their operations might proceed with
even the least probability of success, it was absolutely necessary that but few of the prisoners
should be admitted to the secret. At the same
time, it was impossible for them to make any

progress in their labour, unless they first con-
fided their plan to all the other occupants of the
Gun Room; which was accordingly done. In
this part of the ship, each mess was on terms of
more or less intimacy with those whose little
sleeping enclosures were immediately adjacent to
their own; and the members of each mess frequently interchanged good offices with those in
their vicinity; and borrowed and lent such little
articles as they possessed, like the good house-
wives of a sociable neighbourhood. I never
knew any contention in this apartment during
the whole period of my confinement. Each individual in the Gun Room, therefore, was willing
to assist his comrades, as far as he had the power
to do so. When the proposed plan of escape
was laid before us, although it met the disappro-
bation of by far the greater number, still we
were all perfectly ready to assist those who
thought it practicable.

We, however, described to them the difficul-
ties and dangers which must unavoidably attend
their undertaking; the prospect of detection
while making the aperture, in the immediate

vicinity of such a multitude of idle men, crowded together; a large proportion of whom were always kept awake by their restlessness and sufferings during the night; the little probability that they would be able to travel, undiscovered, on Long Island, even should they succeed in reaching the shore in safety; and, above all, the almost absolute impossibility of obtaining food for their subsistence; as an application for that, to our keepers, would certainly lead to detection. But, notwithstanding all our arguments, a few of them remained determined to make the attempt. Their only reply to our reasoning was, that they must die if they remained; and that nothing worse could befal them if they failed in their undertaking.

One of the most sanguine among the adventurers was a young man named Lawrence, the Mate of a ship from Philadelphia. He was a member of the mess next to my own, and I had formed with him a very intimate acquaintance. He frequently explained his plans to me, and dwelt much upon his hopes of success. But, ardently as I desired to obtain my liberty, and great as were the exertions I would have made, had I seen any probable mode of gaining it, yet it was not my intention to join in this attempt. I nevertheless agreed to assist in the labour of cutting through the planks ; and heartily wished, although I had no hope, that the enterprise might prove successful.

The work was accordingly commenced, and the labourers concealed, by placing a blanket between them and the prisoners without. The counter of the ship was covered with hard oak plank, four inches thick ; and through this we undertook to cut an opening sufficiently large for a man to descend, and to do this with no other tools than our jack knives and a single gimlet.

All the occupants of the Gun Room assisted in this labour, in rotation, — some, in confidence that the plan was practicable ; and the rest, merely for amusement, or for the sake of being employed. Some one of our number was constantly at work ; and we thus continued, wearing a hole through the hard planks, from seam to seam, until at length the solid oak was worn away piecemeal, and nothing remained but a thin sheathing on the outside, which could be cut away at any time, in a few minutes, whenever a suitable opportunity should occur for making the bold attempt to leave the ship.

It had been previously agreed, that those who should first descend through the aperture should drop into the water, and there remain until all those among the inmates of the Gun Room, who chose to make the attempt, could join them, and that the whole band of adventurers should then swim together to the shore, which was about a quarter of a mile from the ship.

A proper time at length arrived. On a very dark and rainy night, the exterior sheathing was cut away ; and at midnight, four of our number, having disencumbered themselves of their clothes, and tied them across their shoulders, were assisted through the opening, and dropped, one after another, into the water.

Ill-fated men ! Our guards had long been acquainted with the enterprise. But, instead of taking any measures to prevent it, they had permitted us to go on with our labour, keeping a

vigilant watch for the moment of our projected
escape, in order to gratify their bloodthirsty
wishes.   No other motive than this could have
prompted them to the course which they pursued.   A boat was in waiting, under the ship's
quarter, manned with rowers and a party of the
guards.   They maintained a perfect silence after
hearing the prisoners drop from the opening;
until, having ascertained that no more would
probably descend, they pursued the swimmers,
whose course they could easily follow by the
sparkling of the water, — an effect always produced by the agitation of the waves in a stormy
night.

We were all profoundly silent in the Gun
Room, after the departure of our companions,
and in anxious suspense as to the issue of their
adventure.   In a few minutes we were startled
by the report of a gun, which was instantly succeeded by a quick and scattering fire of musketry.   In the darkness of the night, we could
not see the unfortunate victims, but could distinctly hear their shrieks and cries for mercy.

The noise of the firing had alarmed the pris-

oners generally ; and the report of the attempted
escape, and its defeat, ran like wildfire through
the gloomy and crowded dungeons of the hulk,
and produced much commotion among the whole
body of the prisoners. In a few moments the
gratings were raised, and the guards descended,
bearing a naked and bleeding man, whom they
placed in one of the bunks ; and having left a
piece of burning candle by his side, they again
ascended to the deck, and secured the gratings.

Information of this circumstance soon reached
the Gun Room ; and myself, with several others
of our number, succeeded in making our way
through the crowd to the bunks. The wounded
man was my friend Lawrence. He was severely
injured in many places, and one of his arms had
been nearly severed from his body by the stroke
of a cutlass. This, he said, was done in wanton
barbarity, while he was crying for mercy, with
his hand on the gunwale of the boat. He was
too much exhausted to answer any of our questions, and uttered nothing further, except a single
enquiry respecting the fate of Nelson, one of his
fellow-adventurers. This we could not answer.

Indeed, what became of the rest, we never knew. They were probably all murdered in the water.

This was the first time that I had ever seen a light between decks. The piece of candle had been left by the side of the bunk in order to produce an additional effect upon the prisoners. Many had been suddenly awakened from their slumbers, and had crowded round the bunk where the sufferer lay. The effect of the partial light upon his bleeding and naked limbs, and upon the pale and haggard countenances and tattered garments of the wild and crowded groups by which he was surrounded, was horrid beyond description.

We could render the sufferer but little assistance; being only able to furnish him with a few articles of apparel, and to bind a handkerchief around his head. His body was completely covered and his hair filled with clotted blood; we had not the means of washing the gore from his wounds during the night. We had seen many die; but to view this wretched man expiring in that situation, where he had been placed beyond

29

the reach of surgical aid, merely to strike us with terror, was dreadful.

The gratings were not removed at the usual hour in the morning, but we were all kept below until ten o'clock. This mode of punishment had now become habitual with our keepers, and we were all frequently detained between decks until a late hour in the day, in revenge for the most trifling occurrence. This cruelty never failed to produce the torments arising from heat and thirst, with all their attendant miseries.

The immediate object of our tyrants having been answered by leaving Mr. Lawrence below in that situation, they promised, in the morning, that he should have the assistance of a Surgeon; but this promise was not fulfilled. The prisoners rendered him every attention in their power. They washed and dressed his wounds; but in vain. Mortification soon commenced; he became delirious and died.

No inquiry was made by our keepers respecting his situation. They evidently left him thus to suffer, in order that the sight of his agonies might deter the rest of the prisoners from following his example.

We received not the least reprimand for this transaction. The aperture was again filled up with plank, and made perfectly secure ; and no similar attempt to escape was made, at least so long as I remained on board.

It was always in our power to knock down the guards and throw them overboard. But this would have been of no avail. If we had done so, and have effected our escape to Long Island, it would have been next to impossible for us to have proceeded any farther, among the number of troops there quartered. Of these there were several regiments ; and among them the regiment of Refugees, before mentioned, who were vigilant in the highest degree, and would have been delighted at the opportunity of apprehending and returning us to our dungeons.

There were, however, several instances of individuals making their escape. One, in particular, I well recollect. James Pitcher, one of the crew of the *Chance*, was placed on the sick-list, and conveyed to Blackwell's Island. He effected his escape from thence to Long Island; from which, after having used the greatest precaution, he contrived to cross the Sound, and arrived safe at home. He is now one of the three survivors of that vessel's crew.

CHAPTER XVIII.

MEMORIAL TO GEN. WASHINGTON.

" The body maddened by the spirit's pain,
" The wild, wild working of the breast and brain,
" The haggard eye, that horror widened, sees
" Death take the start of sorrow and disease ;
" Here, such were seen and heard : — so close at hand,
" A cable's length had reached them from the land ;
" Yet farther off than ocean ever bore ; —
" Eternity between them and the shore ! "

W. READ.

NOTWITHSTANDING the destroying pestilence
which was now raging to a degree hitherto unknown on board, new companies of victims were
continually arriving ; so that, although the mortality was very great, our numbers were increasing daily. Thus situated, and seeing no prospect of our liberation by exchange, we began to

30

despair, and to believe that our certain fate was rapidly approaching.

One expedient was at length proposed among us, and adopted. We petitioned General Clinton, who was then in command of the British forces at New York, for leave to transmit a memorial to General Washington, describing our deplorable situation, and requesting his interference in our behalf. We further desired that our memorial might be examined by the British General, and if approved by him, that it might be carried by one of our number to General Washington.

Our petition was laid before the British commander by the Commissary of Prisoners, and was granted. We received permission to choose three from our number, to whom was promised a passport, with leave to proceed immediately on their embassy.

Our choice was accordingly made, and I had the satisfaction to find that two of those elected were from among the former officers of the *Chance*, Capt. Aborn, and our Surgeon, Mr. Joseph Bowen.

The Memorial was soon completed, and signed, in the name of all the prisoners, by a committee appointed for that purpose. It contained an account of the extreme wretchedness of our condition, and stated, that although we were sensible that the subject was one over which General Washington had no direct control, as it was not usual for soldiers to be exchanged for seamen, and his authority not extending to the marine department of the American service; yet still, although it might not be in his power to effect our exchange, we hoped that he would be able to devise some means to lighten or relieve our sufferings.

Our messengers were further charged with a verbal communication for General Washington, which, for obvious reasons, was not included in the written memorial. They were directed to state, in a manner more circumstantial than we had dared to write, the peculiar horrors of our situation; to describe the miserable food and putrid water on which we were doomed to subsist; and finally to assure the General, that in case he could effect our release, we would agree to enter the American service, as soldiers, and remain during the war. Thus instructed, our messengers departed.

We waited, in alternate hope and fear, the event of their mission. Most of our number who were natives of the Eastern States were strongly impressed with the idea that some means would be devised for our relief, after such a representation of our condition should have been made. This class of the prisoners, indeed, felt most interested in the success of the application; for many of the sufferers appeared to give themselves but little trouble respecting it; and some, among the foreigners, did not even know that such an application had been made, or that it had ever been in contemplation. The long endurance of their privations had rendered them almost indifferent to their fate; and they appeared to look forward to death as the only probable termination of their captivity.

In a few days, our messengers returned to New York, with a letter from General Washington, addressed to the committee of the prisoners who had signed the memorial. The pris-

oners were all summoned to the spar-deck,
where this letter was read. Its purport was as
follows : — That he had perused our communication, and had received with due consideration
the account which our messengers had laid before him ; that he viewed our situation with a
high degree of interest; and that although our
application (as we had stated) was made in relation to a subject over which he had no direct
control, yet that it was his intention to lay our
Memorial before Congress ; and that in the
mean time we might be assured that no exertion on his part should be spared which could
tend to a mitigation of our sufferings.

He observed to our messengers, during their
interview, that our long detention in confinement was owing to a combination of circumstances, against which it was very difficult, if not
impossible, to provide. That, in the first place,
but little exertion was made on the part of our
countrymen to secure and detain their British
prisoners for the purposes of exchange ; many
of the British seamen being captured by priva-
teers, on board which, as he understood, it was a

common practice for them to enter as seamen ;
and that when this was not the case, they were
usually set at liberty, as soon as the privateer
arrived in port, — as neither the owners nor the
town or state where they were landed would be
at the expense of their confinement and mainte-
nance ; and that the officers of the General Government only took charge of those seamen who
were captured by the vessels in the public service.   All which circumstances combined to render the number of British prisoners, at all times,
by far too small for a regular and equal exchange.

General Washington also transmitted to our
committee copies of letters which he had sent to
General Clinton and to the Commissary of Prisoners, which were also read to us.   He therein
expressed an ardent desire that a general exchange of prisoners might be effected ; and if
this could not be accomplished, he wished that
something might be done to lessen the weight of
our sufferings ; that if it was absolutely necessary that we should be confined on the water, he
desired that we might at least be removed to

clean ships. He added, if the Americans should
be driven to the necessity of placing the British
prisoners in situations similar to our own, similar
effects must be the inevitable result; and that he
therefore hoped they would afford us better
treatment, from motives of humanity. He concluded by saying, that as a correspondence on
the subject had thus begun between them, he ardently wished it might eventually result in the
liberation of the unfortunate men whose situation
had called for its commencement.

Our three messengers did not return on board
as prisoners, but were allowed to remain on parole at Flatbush, on Long Island.

We soon found an improvement in our fare.
The bread which we received was of a better
quality, and we were furnished with butter instead of rancid oil. An awning was provided,
and a windsail furnished to conduct fresh air between the decks during the day. But of this we
were always deprived at night, when we most
needed it, as the gratings must always be fastened over the hatchways; and I presume that
our keepers were fearful, if it was allowed to
remain, we might use it as a means of escape.

We were, however, obliged to submit to all our privations; consoling ourselves only with the faint hope, that the favourable change in our situation, which we had observed for the last few days, might lead to something still more beneficial, although we saw but little prospect of escaping from the raging pestilence, except through the immediate interposition of Divine Providence, or by a removal from the scene of contagion.

CHAPTER XIX.

THE EXCHANGE.

"The captive raised his slow and sullen eye;
"He knew no friend, nor deemed a friend was nigh;
"Till the sweet tones of Pity touched his ears,
"And Mercy bathed his bosom with her tears.
"Strange were those tones, to him, those tears were strange;
"He wept, and wondered at the mighty change."

*   *   *   *   *

"Like Peter, sleeping in his chains, he lay;
"The angel came, and night was turned to day;
"'Arise!'—his fetters fall; his slumbers flee;
"He wakes to life; he springs to liberty!"

MONTGOMERY.

SOON after Capt. Aborn had been permitted to go to Long Island on his parole, he sent a message on board the *Jersey*, informing us that his parole had been extended so far as to allow his return home, but that he should visit us previous to his departure. He requested our First Lieutenant, Mr. John Tillinghast, to provide a list of the names of those captured in the *Chance* who had died, and also a list of the survivors, noting where each survivor was then confined, whether on board the *Jersey*, or one of the Hospital Ships.

He also requested that those of our number who desired to write to their friends at home, would have their letters ready for delivery to him, whenever he should come on board. The occupants of the Gun Room, and such of the other prisoners as could procure the necessary materials, were, therefore, soon busily engaged in writing as particular descriptions of our situation as they thought it prudent to do, without the risk of the destruction of their letters, as we were always obliged to submit our writing for inspection, previous to its being allowed to pass from the ship. We, however, afterwards regretted that on this occasion our descriptions were not more minute, as these letters were not examined.

The next day, Capt. Aborn came on board, accompanied by several other persons who had also been liberated on parole ; but they came no

nearer to the prisoners than the head of the
gangway-ladder, and passed through the door of
the barricado to the quarter-deck. This was
perhaps a necessary precaution against the contagion, as they were more liable to be affected
by it than if they had always remained on board;
but we were much disappointed at not having an
opportunity to speak to them. Our letters were
delivered to Capt. Aborn by our Lieutenant,
through whom he sent us assurances of his determination to do everything in his power for our
relief; and that if a sufficient number of British
prisoners could be procured, every survivor of
his vessel's crew should be exchanged; and if
this could not be effected, we might depend on
receiving clothing, and such other necessary articles as could be sent for our use.

About this time some of the sick were sent
ashore on Blackwell's Island. This was considered a great indulgence. I endeavoured to
obtain leave to join them by feigning sickness,
but did not succeed. The removal of the sick
was a great relief to us, as the air was less foul
between decks, and we had more room for mo-

tion. Some of the bunks were removed, and the sick were carried on shore, as soon as their condition was known. Still, however, the pestilence did not abate on board, as the weather was extremely warm. In the day time the heat was excessive, but at night it was intolerable.

But we lived on hope, knowing that in all probability our friends at home had, ere then, been apprized of our condition, and that some relief might perhaps be soon afforded us.

Such was our situation, when, one day, a short time before sunset, we descried a sloop approaching us, with a white flag at her mast-head; and knew, by that signal, that she was a Cartel; and from the direction in which she came, supposed her to be from some of the Eastern States. She did not approach near enough to satisfy our curiosity, until we were ordered below for the night.

Long were the hours of that night to the survivors of our crew. Slight as was the foundation on which our hopes had been raised, we had clung to them as our last resource. No sooner were the gratings removed in the morning, than we were all upon deck, gazing at the Cartel.

Her deck was crowded with men, whom we supposed to be British prisoners. In a few minutes they began to enter the Commissary's boats, and proceeded to New York.

In the afternoon a boat from the Cartel came alongside the hulk, having on board the Commissary of Prisoners; and by his side sat our townsman, Capt. William Corey, who came on board with the joyful information that the sloop was from Providence, with English prisoners, to be exchanged for the crew of the *Chance.* The number which she had brought was forty; being more than sufficient to redeem every survivor of our crew then on board the *Jersey.*

I immediately began to prepare for my departure. Having placed the few articles of clothing which I possessed in a bag (for, by one of our by-laws, no prisoner, when liberated, could remove his chest), I proceeded to dispose of my other property on board; and after having made sundry small donations of less value, I concluded by giving my tin kettle to one of my friends, and to another the remnant of my cleft of firewood.

33

I then hurried to the upper deck, in order to be ready to answer to my name, well knowing that I should hear no second call, and that no delay would be allowed.

The Commissary and Capt. Corey were standing together on the quarter-deck; and as the list of names was read, our Lieutenant, Mr. Tillinghast, was directed to say whether the person called was one of the crew of the *Chance*. As soon as this assurance was given, the individual was ordered to pass down the accommodation-ladder into the boat. Cheerfully was the word " *here !* " responded by each survivor as his name was called. My own turn at length came, and the Commissary pointed to the boat. I never moved with a lighter step, for that moment was the happiest of my life. In the excess and overflowing of my joy, I forgot, for a while, the detestable character of the Commissary himself; and even, Heaven forgive me, bestowed a bow upon him as I passed.

We took our stations in the boat in silence. No congratulations were heard among us. Our feelings were too deep for utterance. For my own part, I could not refrain from bursting into tears of joy.

Still there were intervals when it seemed impossible that we were in reality without the limits of the old *Jersey*. We dreaded the idea that some unforeseen event might still detain us ; and shuddered with the apprehension that we might yet be returned to our dungeons.

When the Cartel arrived, the surviving number of our crew on board the *Jersey* was but thirty-five. This fact being well known to Mr. Tillinghast, and finding that the Cartel had brought forty prisoners, he allowed five of our companions in the Gun Room to answer to the names of the same number of our crew who had died ; and having disguised themselves in the garb of common seamen, they passed unsuspected.

It was nearly sunset when we had all arrived on board the Cartel. So sooner had the exchange been completed than the Commissary left us, with our prayers that we might never behold him more. I then cast my eyes towards the hulk, as the horizontal rays of the setting sun glanced on her polluted sides, where, from the bends upwards, filth of every description had been permitted to accumulate for years ; and the feelings of disgust which the sight occasioned are indescribable. The multitude on her spar-deck and forecastle were in motion, and in the act of descending for the night ; presenting the same appearance that met my sight, when, near-ly five months before, I had, at the same hour, approached her as a prisoner.

CHAPTER XX.

THE CARTEL.

" At length returned unto my native shore,
" How changed I find those scenes which pleased before.
" In sickly ships, what num'rous hosts confined,
" At once their lives and liberties resigned.
" In dreary dungeons, woful scenes have passed ;
" Long in tradition shall the story last :
" As long as Spring renews the flowery wood,
" Or Summer's breezes curl the yielding flood."

FRENEAU.

" Down, Rebels; down ! " was the insulting mandate by which we had usually been sent below for the night; and now, as we stood on the deck of the Cartel, watching the setting sun, I could hardly persuade myself that I should not soon hear that unfeeling order shouted forth by some ruffian sentinel behind me.

34

During the evening, every thing around us contributed to our gratification. It was a pleasure to us even to look at the lighted candles; for, except on the night of the attempted escape, described in a former Chapter, we had not seen any thing of the kind for months. We derived enjoyment from gazing at the stars, not one of which we had seen, in its zenith, since our capture, having never been permitted to look abroad in the night, except through the massy gratings or iron bars of our prison.

We had no desire for sleep; and the whole night was spent in conversation, during which I learned the particular circumstances in relation to our exchange.

On his arrival at Providence, Capt. Aborn had lost no time in making the details of our sufferings publicly known; and a feeling of deep commiseration was excited among our fellow citizens. Messrs. Clarke & Nightingale, the former owners of the *Chance*, in conjunction with other gentlemen, expressed their determination to spare no exertion or expense necessary to procure our liberation. It was found that forty British prisoners were, at that time, in Boston. These were immediately procured, and marched to Providence, where a sloop, owned and commanded by a Capt. Gladding of Bristol, was chartered to proceed with the prisoners forthwith to New York, that they might be exchanged for an equal number of our crew. Capt. Corey was appointed as an Agent, to effect the exchange, and to receive us from the *Jersey ;* and having taken on board a supply of good provisions and water, he hastened to our relief. He received much assistance, in effecting his object, from our townsman, Mr. John Creed, at that time Deputy-Commissary of Prisoners. I do not recollect the exact day of our deliverance, but think it was early in the month of October, 1782.

The sun rose brightly on the morning after our exchange. We spent the time, while our breakfast was preparing, in viewing once more the detested place of our long confinement ; and while the prisoners were crowding on deck, we could occasionally discern among them the figures of some of our former messmates. We could not but compare their situation with our own; and sweet as was the taste to us of wholesome food, gladly would we have relinquished our repast, could we have sent it to them.

Our plentiful breakfast produced a great effect upon our spirits. We soon began to think and feel that we were, once more, *men*. Our anxiety for the arrival of Capt. Corey from the shore was extreme. At length, about ten o'clock, he came on board, and ordered the sloop to be got under weigh. No windlass nor capstan was necessary for that purpose; for we grasped the cable with our hands, and run the anchor up to the bow in a moment. The sails were rapidly set; and with the wind and tide in our favour, we soon lost sight of the *Jersey*, the Hospital Ships, and the dreaded sand bank of the Wall-about.

We were obliged to pass near the shore of Blackwell's Island, where were several of our crew, who had been sent on shore among the sick. They had learned that the Cartel had arrived from Providence, for the purpose of redeeming the crew of the *Chance*, and expected to be taken on board. Seeing us approaching, they had, in order to cause no delay, prepared for their departure, and stood together on the shore, with their bundles in their hands ; but to their unutterable disappointment and dismay, they saw us pass by. We knew them, and bitterly did we lament the necessity of leaving them behind. We could only wave our hands as we passed ; but they could not return the salutation, and stood, as if petrified with horror, like statues, fixed immovably to the earth, until we had vanished from their sight.

I have since seen and conversed with one of these unfortunate men, who afterwards made his escape. He informed me that their removal from the *Jersey* to the Island, was productive of the most beneficial effects upon their health, and that they had been exulting at the improvement in their condition ; but their terrible disappointment overwhelmed them with despair. They then considered their fate inevitable ; believing that in a few days they must be again conveyed on board the hulk, there to undergo all the agonies of another death.

35

We were hailed and examined by two guard ships near the Island, but were not long detained. When this was over, and all fear of further detention by our enemies had vanished, we gave way at once to our unrestrained feelings. We breathed a purer air ; it was the air of Freedom. Every countenance was lighted up with smiles, and every heart swelled with expectation. Each hour presented some new and pleasing object, some well-known spot, some peaceful dwelling, or some long remembered spire.

Several of our crew were sick when we entered the Cartel, and the sudden change of air and diet caused some new cases of fever. This we attributed in a great degree to our having partaken too freely of fish and vegetables, — a diet to which we had long been unaccustomed, and with which we were then abundantly supplied. No one, however, died on board the sloop.

One of our number, who was thus seized by the fever, was a young man named Bicknell, of Barrington, Rhode Island. He was unwell when

we left the *Jersey*, and his symptoms indicated
the approaching fever; and when we entered
Narragansett Bay, he was apparently dying.
Being informed that we were in the Bay, he
begged to be taken on deck, or at least to the
hatchway, that he might look once more upon
his native land.   He said that he was sensible of
his condition; that the hand of death was upon
him; but that he was consoled by the thought
that his remains would be decently interred, and
be suffered to rest among those of his friends
and kindred.   I was astonished at the degree of
resignation and composure with which he spoke.
He pointed to his father's house, as we approached
it, and said it contained all that was dear to him
on earth.   He requested to be put on shore.
Our Captain was intimately acquainted with the
family of the sufferer; and, as the wind was
light, we dropped our anchor, and complied with
his request.   He was placed in the boat, where
I took a seat by his side, in order to support
him; and with two boys at the oars, we left the
sloop.   In a few minutes his strength began
rapidly to fail.   He laid his fainting head upon

my shoulder, and said he was going to the shore,
to be buried with his ancestors; that this had
long been his ardent desire; and that God had
heard his prayers. No sooner had we touched
the shore, than one of the boys was sent to in-
form his family of the event. They hastened
to the boat to receive their long lost son and
brother; but we could only give them — his
yet warm, but lifeless corpse.

CHAPTER XXI.

OUR ARRIVAL HOME.

" There is a spot of earth supremely blest,
" A dearer, sweeter spot than all the rest,
" Where man, creation's tyrant, casts aside
" His sword and sceptre, pageantry and pride.
" Here woman reigns; the mother, daughter, wife,
" Strew with fresh flowers the narrow way of life.
" ' Where shall that *land*, that *spot of earth* be found ? '
" Art thou a man ? — a patriot ? — look around :
" Oh, thou shalt find, howe'er thy footsteps roam,
" That land THY COUNTRY, and that spot THY HOME ! "

MONTGOMERY.

AFTER remaining for a few minutes with the
friends of our deceased comrade, we returned to
the sloop, and proceeded up the river. It was
about eight o'clock in the evening when we
reached Providence. There were no quarantine
regulations to detain us ; but as the yellow fever

was raging among us, we took the precaution to anchor in the middle of the stream. It was a beautiful moonlight evening ; and the intelligence of our arrival having spread through the town, the nearest wharf was in a short time crowded with people, drawn together by curiosity, and a desire for information relative to the fate of their friends and connexions. Continual enquiries were made from the anxious crowd on the land, respecting the condition of several different individuals on board. At length the information was given that some of our number were below, sick with the yellow fever. No sooner was this fact announced, than the wharf was totally deserted, and in a few minutes not a human being remained in sight. " The old *Jersey* Fever," as it was called, was well known throughout the whole country. All were acquainted with its terrible effects ; and it was shunned as if its presence was certain destruction.

After the departure of the crowd, the sloop was brought alongside the wharf, and every one who could walk immediately sprang on shore. So great was the dread of the pestilence, and so squalid and emaciated were the figures which we presented, that those among us whose families did not reside in Providence, found it almost impossible to gain admittance into any dwelling. There being at that time no hospital in or near the town, and no preparations having been made for the reception of the sick, they were abandoned for that night. They were, however, supplied in a few hours, with many small articles necessary for their immediate comfort, by the humane people in the vicinity of the wharf.

The friends of the sick who belonged in the vicinity of the town, were immediately informed of our arrival; and in the course of the following day, these were removed from the vessel. For the remainder of the sufferers ample provision was made, through the generous exertions of Messrs. Clark & Nightingale.

Solemn indeed are the reflections which crowd upon my mind, as I review the events which are here recorded. Forty-two years have passed away since this remnant of our ill-fated crew were thus liberated from their wasting captivity.

In that time what changes have taken place.
Of their whole number, but three are now alive.
James Pitcher, Dr. Joseph Bowen, and myself,
are the sole survivors.   Of their officers, I alone
remain.

CONCLUSION.

I CANNOT close these sketches without refer-
ring to the fate of the old *Jersey*. At the expi-
ration of the war, in 1783, the prisoners remaining on board were liberated ; and the hulk being
considered unfit for further use, was abandoned
where she lay. The dread of contagion prevented every one from venturing on board, and
even from approaching her polluted frame. But
the ministers of destruction were at work. Her
planks were soon filled with worms, who, as if
sent to remove this disgrace to the name of
common humanity, ceased not from their labour
until they had penetrated through her decaying
bottom, through which the water rushed in, and
she sunk. With her went down the names of
many thousands of our countrymen, with which
her inner planks and sheathing were literally

covered; for but few of her inmates had ever neglected to add their own names to the almost innumerable catalogue. Could these be counted, some estimate might now be made of the whole number who were there immured; but this record has long since been consigned to eternal oblivion. It is supposed that more men perished on her decks than ever died in any other place of confinement on the face of the earth, in the same number of years.

Notwithstanding the lapse of time, and the consequent decay and dissolution of the remains of the multitudes who were buried on the shore, which were continually washed from the sand and wasted by the elements, when, in the year 1803, the bank at the Wallabout was removed for the purpose of building a Navy Yard, a very great quantity of bones were collected. A memorial was presented to Congress, requesting an appropriation sufficient to defray the expenses necessary for their interment, and for the erection of a suitable Monument upon the spot; but the application was unsuccessful. In the year 1808, the bones were interred under the direc-

tion of the Tammany Society of New York, attended by a solemn funeral procession, in the
presence of a vast concourse of citizens; and the
corner stone of a Monument was laid (to use
the impressive words which are inscribed upon
it), " *in the name of the Spirits of the Departed
Free.*"

APPLEWOOD BOOKS
BRINGING THE PAST ALIVE

TIMELESS ADVICE & ENTERTAINMENT
FROM AMERICANS WHO CAME BEFORE US

George Washington on Manners

Benjamin Franklin on Money

Lydia Maria Child on Raising Children

Henry David Thoreau on Walking

&

Many More Distinctive Classics

Now Available Again

At finer bookstores

& gift shops or from:

APPLEWOOD BOOKS
distributed by
The Globe Pequot Press
Box Q, Chester, CT 06412• (203) 526-9571